GOD
OR MAMMON?

Understanding the Source
and Purpose of
True Kingdom Wealth

AYO AKERELE

ACKNOWLEDGMENTS

I acknowledge the unusual influence of the Holy Spirit in my life and ministry as a teacher and pastor. To Him alone be all the glory. I wholeheartedly dedicate this book to the Holy Spirit, my greatest teacher.

The life and ministry of Pastor Sunday Adelaja in Kiev, Ukraine, has greatly impacted me and the birth of this great piece. I thank God that He gave you to the world. Every nation needs someone like you.

I celebrate the life of God's general and my spiritual father, Bishop Francis Wale Oke, in my life. More than anything else, my desire is that you will finish well and finish strong.

Pastor Derek Schneider has been of immense blessings to me through his History Maker Movement across the nations of the world. The Lord will preserve you and your work in Jesus's mighty name.

To Pastor Michael Samuel, the founder of House of Prayer Ministries in the UK, I owe a big thanks for inspiring me in the birth of this work. He is a great man of God with enormous passion for revival across the nations of the world.

To Pastor Ken Egede, the Zonal Pastor of RCCG, Jesus House Toronto in Canada, I owe a big thanks. He is a true man of love with a large heart to see everyone around him rise to prominence.

Rev. (Dr.) Olive Adelodun and Apostle David Oni have influenced my life tremendously over the years. Your labours of love will not be in vain in Jesus's mighty name.

To all the members and staff of the Voice of the Watchmen Ministries (a.k.a. Rhema for Living Assembly), worldwide, may God bless you richly. You will not labour in vain.

Finally, I acknowledge and celebrate my one and only sweetheart, Omolara Olawunmi, whose support cannot be fully quantified in the pages of this book. Truly, after God, the next best gift in a man's life is his wife. Until death do us part, no one shall take your place as we work together to advance God's kingdom on earth.

INTRODUCTION

Ipleaded with the Lord to save my face from any backlash from the publication of this book. "Dear Lord, I don't want to lose my reputation! Lord this would spoil my brand and throw me into the river of controversy." Such were the words that filled my heart as I struggled with God in a heartfelt negotiation with Him on the subject matter of this book, as if I didn't know that the only fight a man must never win is the fight with God.

One of my mentors, Pastor Sunday Adelaja, has championed a revolution in the nation of Ukraine that is built on taking the kingdom of God to society even in the face of extreme opposition. In a recent conversation with one of his assistants, I was reminded of his stand on matters related to controversies—and the Holy Spirit emboldened me. I gave the Lord a heartfelt promise that I would deliver this message to my generation, even if this costs me my reputation and brand.

But wait a minute, do I have any brand? The only brand I have is the one purchased for me at the foot of the cross by my precious Lord and saviour. Apostle Paul, in Philippians 3:7, said, *"But what things were gain to me, those I counted loss for Christ."* I am therefore ready to lose my brand and reputation, if these would be the seeds for the revival of revelation in the body of Christ towards matters related to the source and purpose of finances in the body of Christ around the world.

Such was my resolve in carrying out with this assignment given to me by my master—to expose the differences between what is God and what is mammon in the financial practices of today's church. Someone once said that finance is the most critical issue of interest to churchgoers in any nation. In other words, we receive the most feedback and responses when money is discussed in the church.

Bible scholars have argued that Jesus spoke about money and material things more than the crucial issues of life and eternity. Could the focus given to money and material things be directly linked to the level of importance heaven attaches to these elements? Why has the present-day church faced such enormous criticism in the areas of its financial dealings? Why has the present-day church lost respect with the world when financial practices are mentioned? Is the passion of church leaders towards finances and wealth accumulation godly, or has Satan secretly crept into the church with the spirit of mammon? Where does God stand in this matter, and what is the Spirit saying to the church in this end time?

Now that we've been inundated with numerous cases of financial mismanagement among church leaders in many parts of the world, including financial misappropriation, wealth accumulation, lack of transparency, and diversion of church funds, where do we go from here? Answers to this question form the basis for this book, in which I take my brethren from around the world, including ministers of the gospel and Christians at large, through a journey of discovery—the discovery of truth as found in the Holy Scriptures.

No man can serve two masters: for either he will hate the one, and love the other; or else he will hold to the one, and despise the other. Ye cannot serve God and mammon. (Matthew 6:24)

The Spirit speaks expressly in this book that there is a difference between what is God's and what is mammon. Probably, what most Christian leaders call God's is largely mammon, and they are completely ignorant of this. The time is now ripe to set the captives free. To open the eyes of many to the truth about the source and purpose of kingdom prosperity. To free men from the chains Satan has used to constrain truth. Ultimately, to separate what is God from what is mammon in the financial practices of the twenty-first-century church of the living God.

CHAPTER ONE

HISTORY AND DEMOGRAPHICS
OF THE CHURCH

Many Bible scholars agree that since the beginning of the twentieth century, the church of Christ has witnessed the emergence of three movements: charismatic, Pentecostal, and neo-charismatic. The history of Pentecostalism dates back to the first century A.D., when the Holy Spirit came upon the apostles in the upper room. Research shows that from around A.D. 96, Clement, the Bishop of Rome, and Ignatius, the Bishop of Antioch, began to document the growth of the Pentecostal movement.

THESE PENTECOSTAL REVIVALS WERE CHARACTERIZED BY A MIGHTY OUTPOURING OF THE HOLY SPIRIT ON YOUNG MEN AND WOMEN WHO WERE USED INCREDIBLY BY GOD TO PERFORM UNUSUAL MIRACLES, SIGNS, AND WONDERS THAT DREW THE ATTENTION OF THE ENTIRE WORLD.

In *The New International Dictionary of Pentecostal Charismatic Movements*, these three movements are characterized by "exuberant worship; emphasis on subjective religious experience and spiritual gifts; [and] claims of supernatural miracles, signs and wonders and mystical life in the spirit."[1] Incidentally, it is difficult

---

[1] Stanley M. Burgess and Edouard M. van der Maas, eds., *The New International Dictionary of Pentecostal and Charismatic Movements* (Grand Rapids, MI: Zondervan, 2003), 290–291.

to ascertain whether any of the authors of this book are actually born-again Christians. However, regardless of their faith, their accounts of the history and attributes of today's church have a far-reaching impact on our understanding of the activities of churches in these last days.

The birth of modern Pentecostalism has been traced to 1901, when a revival broke out at Charles F. Parham's Bethel Bible School. This was followed by the famous Azusa Street revival that occurred between 1906 and 1909. These Pentecostal revivals were characterized by a mighty outpouring of the Holy Spirit on young men and women who were used incredibly by God to perform unusual miracles, signs, and wonders that drew the attention of the entire world. This group of Christians was extremely united in their relationships, and they emphasized a commitment to lives of holiness and purity. According to the accounts of Stanley M. Burgess, these waves of revival later spread to places like Canada, England, Scandinavia, Germany, India, China, Africa, and South America.

...CHARISMATICS DIFFER SLIGHTLY FROM THE PENTECOSTALS IN THAT THEY ARE WIDELY BRANDED AS SUPERNATURALISTIC AND CULTURE-AFFIRMING IN THEIR PERSPECTIVE OF THE CHRISTIAN LIFE.

The charismatic movements share striking similarities with the Pentecostals, as they also emphasize a strong commitment to a life of the spirit and the demonstration of the gifts of the spirit. However, charismatics differ slightly from the Pentecostals in that they are widely branded as supernaturalistic and culture-affirming in their perspective of the Christian life. Conversely, the neo-charismatics are hybrids of the Pentecostals and charismatics in that they also place a strong emphasis on the Holy Spirit, spiritual gifts, sign, wonders, and power encounters, but they often consist of denominations and groups from different cultural backgrounds. Scholars argue that there are about 18,810 independent and indigenous groups and denominations that fall into the neo-charismatic category worldwide.

GLOBAL CHURCH STATISTICS

In a place like Nigeria, the proportions of Christians and churches associated with the Pentecostal, charismatic, and neo-charismatic movements are fifty-one percent, thirty-five percent, and ninety percent respectively. This reveals the prevalence of churches and denominations in Nigeria that are overtly controlled by the cultural orientations of people in different cities, which tends to introduce a lot of doctrinal errors into people's belief systems. It is therefore no wonder that a lot of criticism has been levelled against neo-charismatic churches in Nigeria, most especially in the areas of adulteration of scriptures. The mix of churches and individuals in the Pentecostal, charismatic, and neo-charismatic movements has been extensively researched. The following table outlines the spread of groups and denominations for many other nations in the context of these three movements.

COUNTRIES	PENTECOSTAL (%)	CHARISMATIC (%)	NEO-CHARISMATIC (%)
Nigeria	51	35	90
Ghana	19	20	61
United States	7	16	84
United Kingdom	5	70	25
Canada	11	59	30
Brazil	31	42	26
Australia	6	72	22
South Africa	8	11	81
Kenya	25	21	54
Japan	3	9	88
South Korea	32	27	42
Russia	2	15	82
Ukraine	10	15	76
Zimbabwe	3	5	92
New Zealand	6	71	23

China	0	1	99
Italy	3	82	11
India	4	15	81

Source: Stanley M. Burgess and Edouard M. van der Maas, eds., *The New International Dictionary of Pentecostal and Charismatic Movements* (Grand Rapids, MI: Zondervan, 2003), 290–291.

OTHER STATISTICS

Religions in Africa
- 63% Christians
- 30% Muslims
- 3% Traditional religions

Of the Christians
- 57% Protestant
- 34% Catholic
- 8% Orthodox
- 1% Others[2][3]

More than sixty percent of the nations listed in the above table have more denominations and groups in the neo-charismatic movements than in the other two movements. This demonstrates a very worrisome trend in the establishment of churches and movements with doctrines that can potentially be influenced by human culture, rather than by strict obedience to the word of God as contained in the Holy Scriptures. In fact, almost all African countries surveyed have more members, churches, and denominations in the neo-charismatic movements than in the other two categories.

There can be just one interpretation: many churches in Africa stand the risk of introducing human cultural orientations, human value

[2] Pew-Templeton Global Religious Futures Project, "Sub-Sharan Africa." Date of access: May 26, 2016 (http://www.globalreligiousfutures.org/regions/sub-saharan-africa).

[3] Pew Research Center, "Global Christianity: A Report on the Size and Distribution of the World's Christian Population." December 19, 2011 (http://www.pewforum.org/2011/12/19/global-christianity-exec/).

systems, and secular ways of doing things into biblical doctrines. Of course, the same trend is visible in churches in the United States, Asia, and in certain part of Europe including Russia and the Ukraine. It is not surprising that many churches in these countries have been involved in numerous cases of erroneous teachings, doctrinal errors, and the adulteration of the Bible.

One of the most disastrous outcomes of this trend is the covert introduction of the spirit of mammon into the church of God. This will be critically examined in the light of Scripture as we proceed.

In 2000, a survey was conducted on the total income of churches worldwide from 1900 to 2003, and projected to 2025. The total giving of members was also summarized. The table below helps to explain the relationship between these two entities.

INCOME/YEAR	1900 ($US)	1970 ($US)	1995 ($US)	2000 ($US)	2025 ($US)
Total annual income of all churches worldwide	250 million	157 billion	1.280 trillion	1.550 trillion	2.4 trillion
Total annual giving to Christian causes worldwide	7 million	3 billion	25 billion	30 billion	46 billion

Source: Stanley M. Burgess and Edouard M. van der Maas, eds., *The New International Dictionary of Pentecostal and Charismatic Movements* (Grand Rapids, MI: Zondervan, 2003), 290–291.

Some more recent statistics on the total global income of church members have also been presented in other fora. For example, it's been widely reported that more than $15 trillion have been received by churches worldwide in offerings, donations and probably, business activities of churches.

CATEGORIES	AMOUNT ($US)
Total personal income of church members	15.5 trillion
Giving to Christian causes	280 billion
Church embezzlement (reported versions)	16 billion
Income of global foreign missions	16 billion

Source: Southern Nazarene University, "Statistics: The 21st-Century World." Date of access: May 2, 2016 (https://home.snu.edu/~hculbert/world.htm).

SAMPLE STATEMENT OF OPERATIONS FOR A U.S.-BASED CHURCH

	2013	2014
Total Income	$2,301,499	$2,285,483
Donations	$1,610,845	$1,493,150
Rental Income	$19,538	$24,625

The second table reveals that close to seventy percent of the total income of a U.S. church came from donations from its members. The percentage could be greater in many African churches, particularly in churches based in places like Nigeria, Ghana, and South Africa. These statistics do not represent an accurate picture of the true finances of churches, including those within Africa. They have, however, been selected to give readers an idea of the scale and spread of finances at the disposal of churches in different parts of the world.

Quite certainly, the level of donations and giving of church members in churches such as in Nigeria represents a vast proportion of the total annual income of churches in these countries. One striking observation is that churches across the globe must be doing things to generate income apart from the donations of their members, for there is a wide discrepancy between the annual income of churches and annual giving of their members.

Another important factor to consider is the fact that this research was conducted more than ten years ago. It is therefore possible for today's reality not to have been captured in the findings. My perception about this finding is that there is enormous wealth in the church, but no organized finance or central bank accounts. What an indictment! This could be the reason behind the untold financial recklessness of many preachers.

My assignment here is simple: to uncover the sources and purpose of money in the church of Christ. Gaps in the financial practices of many church movements will be examined in the light of Scripture.

SUMMARY OF CHAPTER ONE

1. The church of Christ is now segmented into the charismatic, Pentecostal, and neo-charismatic movements.
2. The vast majority of African, American, and Asian churches are associated with the neo-charismatic movement.
3. The neo-charismatic movements are characterized by a deep commitment to the Holy Spirit, spiritual gifts, signs, wonders, and power encounters, but they often consist of denominations and groups from different cultural backgrounds.
4. The diverse cultural backgrounds of members of the neo-charismatic movements often present opportunities for the adulteration of the basic doctrines of the Bible with human value systems and human cultural inclinations.
5. There is enormous wealth in the church of Christ worldwide, most of which appears to come from member donations, but a portion comes from other sources that appear to emanate from business-related activities.

It's now important for us to go back to the beginning. How did the early church relate to material things, including raising and spending money for church work? What were their approaches, motivations, and standards, and how do these differ from the practices of many churches today?

All of these questions will be answered in the next section. I intend to critically review the activities of the early church as found in the

Holy Scriptures, and as found in other relevant Bible commentaries and literature. The Holy Spirit is our ultimate guide as we champion a change towards truth and a dismissal of the spirit of mammon in the church of Christ across the globe. Join me as we examine the attributes and dynamics of the financial practices of the early church.

CHAPTER TWO

The Financial Practices of
THE EARLY CHURCH

And the multitude of them that believed were of one heart and of one soul: neither said any of them that ought of the things which he possessed was his own; but they had all things common. (Acts 4:32)

The heart of the early church was so closely knit together that we begin to wonder where things have gone wrong with the present-day church. I am one of those progressives who doesn't see the cup as half-empty, but as half-full. In other words, I'm not a pessimist out there to ridicule the church of Christ. However, my assignment is very simple: to expose the errors in the source and use of finances in the church, using this as the basis for redirecting the focus of the church to the appropriate use of money.

As soon as Jesus departed from this world, leaving the apostles to continue with the transformation He instituted, the leadership of the church was characterized by one thing—love. This love was so contagious that the apostles were called Christians for the first time in Antioch. Not because they demanded to be branded Christians, but because society could relate their relationship to one another and the world with that of Jesus. This reminds me of a saying attributed to Francis of Assisi: "Preach the gospel *at all times*; when necessary, use words." Our actions speak louder and stronger than our words.

The apostles perfectly exemplified the nature and character of Jesus. If Jesus laid out the standards that the early church followed, is it not appropriate to chronicle specific case studies in Jesus's ministry where

He requested and used resources? I think this would be a good starting point, as we would have sufficient basis to juxtapose the attributes of the first church with those of Jesus when He was physically on earth.

JESUS'S CONTINUATION OF THE BEATITUDES
Jesus's first statement about money is explicitly made in Matthew 6:1–4. In these four verses, Jesus set out a kingdom practice relating to giving money to charitable causes. Jesus makes it clear:

> *Take heed that ye do not your alms before men, to be seen of them: otherwise ye have no reward of your Father which is in heaven.*
>
> *Therefore when thou doest thine alms, do not sound a trumpet before thee, as the hypocrites do in the synagogues and in the streets, that they may have glory of men. Verily I say unto you, They have their reward.*
>
> *But when thou doest alms, let not thy left hand know what thy right hand doeth: that thine alms may be in secret: and thy Father which seeth in secret himself shall reward thee openly.* (Matthew 6:1–4).

The New Testament was translated from Greek. The Greek word for "alms" is *Eleos*. According to Strong's Greek dictionary, this means "compassionateness, i.e. (as exercised towards the poor) beneficence, or (concretely) a benefaction–alms."[4] The striking context in which this word is used is towards the poor. Almsgiving is therefore a practice for providing for the need of materially poor people.

The above verses contain striking kingdom principles laid out by our master Himself. Jesus's attitude and perspective about money, as it relates to how it should be used, are clearly enumerated. According to Jesus;
- Almsgiving is a kingdom practice.
- There is no reference to giving alms only to Christians. Jesus used the word "men," and this refers to giving alms to every category of humans as long as there is a need for it.

---

[4] Bible Hub, "1654. eleémosuné." Date of access: May 26, 2016 (http://biblehub.com/greek/1654.htm).

- For almsgiving, it is not a matter of if, but a matter of when. As New Testament believers, we must be involved in charities.
- Almsgiving, or donating to charitable causes, must not be done to attract undue attention from men. As much as it is possible, we must do it as a private kingdom service to God.
- God rewards charitable practices.

Now, Jesus didn't specify whether almsgiving must only come in the form of giving money alone. I presume that money, materials, and other gifts that help to meet the needs of men qualify as alms before God.

THE SERMON ON THE MOUNTAIN ABOUT POSSESSIONS

Jesus's second attempt at revealing His will about money and material resources is explicitly discussed in Matthew 6:11–34. The first part of these scriptures provides the master's blueprint for the management of material blessings, both in terms of our mindset as Christians towards acquiring resources and how these resources must be eventually used. In verse 11, Jesus mentions that we must pray to God to *"[g]ive us… our daily bread."* A casual reader will think Jesus was teaching us not to be strategic in life, not to plan for the future. No, sir. Jesus was trying to discourage the pressure of worrying about the future by focusing our attention on solving problems as they arise. Many Christians are too worried about tomorrow, which is the very reason why they do all they can to acquire financial resources by crook and by hook. If you read other statements from Jesus in the gospels and balance them with the accounts of the apostles in the epistles, you will see that Jesus never endorses laziness and foolishness. But believers and preachers in general must learn to balance their approach to solving

> MANY CHRISTIANS ARE TOO WORRIED ABOUT TOMORROW, WHICH IS THE VERY REASON WHY THEY DO ALL THEY CAN TO ACQUIRE FINANCIAL RESOURCES BY CROOK AND BY HOOK.

future problems in a way that doesn't compromise solutions to today's affairs.

Jesus clearly forbids the attitude of *"laying up"* material things (Matthew 6:19). This scripture has been a subject of contention among many believers. Perhaps we should review the meaning of this verse from other versions of the Bible. The Common English Bible states,

> *Stop collecting treasures* for your own benefit on earth, *where moth and rust eat them and where thieves break in and steal them.* (CEB, emphasis added)

Could anything be clearer than this? The Good News Bible reads like this:

> *Do not store up riches for yourselves here on earth, where moths and rust destroy, and robbers break in and steal.* (Matthew 6:19, GNT)

Verse 20 describes the master's heart and attitude towards the management of riches and resources with an exact opposite approach to the first approach. The riches must be stored in heaven. What does it mean to store up riches? It's an attitude reflected in a greedy penchant for acquiring wealth and resources without making provision to dispense such riches for the service of the kingdom and humanity in general.

In practice, the Dead Sea is widely reputed for collecting water from several sources without releasing it. The Red Sea is an exact opposite. Are you a Red Sea or a Dead Sea? We will deal more about this in subsequent chapters.

From Matthew 6:24–34, we can again see the attitude of the master towards money and resources. We will deal with the concept of mammonism in subsequent sections. However, the central focus of Jesus in the other verses was on a single word: worry. No desire for resources or money justifies any reason to live in worry. You must not worry about the lack of money or the lack of other resources. Thus, in this section, the following stands out.

- You must not worry about the lack of money or the lack of any other resource.

- You must not acquire money or resources for the sole purpose of storing them up, but for the purpose of using them to extend God's kingdom on earth to all categories of people, regardless of their religion.

- A preacher of the gospel or a Christian brother or sister must not be overwhelmed by the need of the future in a manner that destroys the capacity to get today's needs met. Simply put, Christians must be focused at solving money problems from the present to the future and not from the future to the present.

- No financial need, regardless of how big and important, is permitted to cause a Christian to live in worry. You must not worry about money!

THE SENDING FORTH OF JESUS'S DISCIPLES

The third reference to Jesus's attitude about money is described in His instructions to the twelve apostles in the Matthew 10:

> *Heal the sick, cleanse the lepers, raise the dead, cast out devils:* freely ye have received, freely give. *Provide* neither gold, nor silver, nor brass in your purses... (Matthew 10:8–9, emphasis added)

ANY PREACHER OR CHRISTIAN WHO MERCHANDISES THE POWER OF GOD IS CERTAINLY WORKING OUTSIDE THE WILL OF GOD AND THERE ARE CONSEQUENCES FOR THIS.

These were the master's third statements on money and resources in the gospels, which are highly instructive. If Jesus should be the author and finisher of our faith, we must listen to what He has to say about every issue of life. The above scriptures tell us that the master Himself does not endorse merchandising the power of God. No preacher or Christian must make profit from the power of God. In other words, demand for gratification as a condition for dispensing the power of God is totally against the will of our master. Secondly, in the same verse, Jesus is firmly against building our confidence and hopes on finances as preconditions to preaching the gospel at any level.

If the author and finisher of our faith isn't happy with these two approaches to ministry and the preaching of the gospel, why should any preacher endorse such practices? Any preacher or Christian who merchandises the power of God is certainly working outside the will of God and there are consequences for this. The same applies to anyone who craves the availability of financial resources as a precondition to preaching the gospel. Thus, what are the instructions of our masters towards finances and resources in general from these verses?

- No preacher of the gospel or Christian must merchandise the anointing and power of God
- No preacher of the gospel or Christian must be motivated by the love for financial reward as a precondition to offering any spiritual assistance to anybody. In other words, no preacher is permitted to request financial reward prior to offering spiritual assistance to people
- No one called by God into the ministry of the gospel must make the availability of financial resources the precondition to answering and running with the call.
- Since there must be a purse, it is certain that God will provide the financial resources to fill up the purse after the call has been answered.

Sadly, a lot of things are going on in the body of Christ that leave nothing to be desired in being a preacher of the gospel. A certain popular Pentecostal church in Nigeria, one which I will call neo-charismatic, has been charging church members a gate fee for attending New Year crossover services. It has happened a couple of times and has generated enormous contention in the body of Christ in Nigeria. The majority of Christians in Nigeria are opposed to this practice. Certainly, this is very wrong and unjustified. This church is reputed to have a seating capacity between fifteen and twenty thousand, and prospective attendants were required to pay one thousand naira to be allowed to sit in the auditorium. This generated a minimum of fifteen million naira for the church apart from offerings and other special donations. This is a sacrilege and totally against the master's instructions. It is an aberration and a sin against God. We enjoin all who practice this to stop and repent. Otherwise, the judgement of God will soon fall on them. It is only a matter of time.

Jesus's attitude to finances and other resources are also clearly stated in the four canonical gospels. In Matthew 21:12–13, Jesus emphasized that regardless of the amount of money involved and the associated benefits, the temple of God must be accorded its respect and used solely for what it is meant for. You and I are the New Testament temple of the Holy Spirit. Giving our bodies to prayer is more important to God than giving our bodies to making money. This appears to be contradictory to some people's mindsets.

Certainly, God is interested in our finances, and He obviously takes delight in our prosperity. However, our priorities must be set aright. You can't be a prayerless Christian and devote your entire life to making money and expect to develop into a mature son of God. In that context, money is irrelevant if you are not a praying Christian. God is interested in raising spiritually responsible children who will understand how to set their priorities aright.

The master's attitude about money is also explored in Matthew 25:14–30, the parable of the talents. Three people were given different amounts of money by their master, and after a while the master asked them to give account of their stewardship. Those who multiplied the money were called good and faithful servants.

Bible teacher Derek Prince taught on this chapter and emphasized the need for us to consider the master's yardstick for performance measurement. The verse does not say "good and successful," but rather "good and faithful," meaning that faithfulness in matters of money is far more important to God than the success of making money. You can successfully achieve a four hundred percent profit in business, yet be unfaithful in meeting specific expectations. This clearly tells us that rather than labouring towards becoming successful at the expense of being faithful, we must seek to be both successful and faithful.

Sometimes these two don't go together easily, but with the help of the Holy Spirit, they can comfortably be combined.

Jesus had many other encounters on issues related to money and financial resources, including his encounter with the woman with the widow's mite, the encounter with the Pharisee who asked him about paying taxes to Caesar, and his instructions to Peter to fish for money in the mouth of a fish. We won't discuss all of these cases in much detail. However, one that stands out occurs in John 6:1–6. Jesus needed to feed at least five thousand people, minus children and women, and He asked one of His disciples about where they could find bread.

When Jesus then lifted up his eyes, and saw a great company come unto him, he saith unto Philip, Whence shall we buy bread, that these may eat? And this he said to prove him: for he himself knew what he would do.

Philip answered him, Two hundred pennyworth of bread is not sufficient for them, that every one of them may take a little.

One of his disciples, Andrew, Simon Peter's brother, saith unto him, There is a lad here, which hath five barley loaves, and two small fishes: but what are they among so many?

And Jesus said, Make the men sit down. Now there was much grass in the place. So the men sat down, in number about five thousand.

And Jesus took the loaves; and when he had given thanks, he distributed to the disciples, and the disciples to them that were set down; and likewise of the fishes as much as they would. (John 6:5–11)

From these scriptures emerge crucial principles of a faith-based relationship with God regarding money:
- Jesus emphasized compassion for people above one's lack of financial resources.
- Jesus emphasized the solution to the need more than the source of the solution.

• Rather than merchandising the anointing to collect from people, Jesus showed that the opposite must be done. We must use the anointing to create solutions to the problems of people.

Jesus is our ultimate role model when examining matters related to the source and ultimate use of finances. Next to Jesus are the standards laid down by the apostles in the epistles.

We have examined several of Jesus's encounters with specific situations that either required Him to use money, seek money, or teach people about the best attitude towards money and other vital resources. We will now examine how the early church related to money. The two key questions in my heart are:

• How did the apostles raise finances for their ministry work?
• How did the apostles use finances in their ministry?

You will be surprised that there is perfect synergy between the principles Jesus taught in all of the cases we mentioned earlier and the practices of the apostles in the book of Acts.

THE ATTITUDE OF THE APOSTLES TOWARDS FINANCES

The first time the finances of the apostles are mentioned is in Acts 4:32:

And the multitude of them that believed were of one heart and of one soul: neither said any of them that ought of the things which he possessed was his own; but they had all things common.

Inside this scripture is a profound principle of the kingdom as it relates to the relationship between Christians and resources in the church of God. Look at the last two sentences: *"neither said any of them that ought of the things which he possessed was his own; but they had all things common."* The King James translation often introduces confusion, so let's examine these sentences in the light of other translations. Read with me from the New Century Translation:

All those in the group acted as though their private property belonged to everyone in the group. In fact, they shared everything. (Acts 4:32, NCV)

How clearer could a scripture be? Do we need to fast and pray for God to help us understand what this means? I don't think so. It's as clear as crystal. The relationship between brothers and sisters in the early church was so cordial that nobody laid claim to any of their resources. The words "This is mine" were not in their vocabulary. "I laboured hard to get to where I am" wasn't found in their dialect. They perfectly epitomized the description of love as explained and taught by the master. They had a sense of unity and bonding. In fact, they perfectly epitomized Jesus's blueprint for true discipleship:

By this shall all men know that ye are my disciples, if ye have love one to another. (John 13:35)

This is nothing short of love! The early church was a symbol of love. Of course, they had their own challenges and didn't represent a flawless group of people. They missed it at times and disappointed the leadership of the church. Paul's epistles to the Corinthians reflect some of the challenges faced by the early church. But in matters relating to the management of resources, particularly finances and assets, they fared well.

This isn't an attempt to use the men who lived then as standards for us today. This book isn't people-based, but principle-based. We are extracting the principles they practiced. This reminds me of what a Hebrew school once said: "Eat the fish and leave the bone." We are eating the fish of their love principles, and leaving the bones of their failures and shortcomings.

Love was at the centre of it all. Finances weren't greedily pursued at the expense of neglecting the concerns of other people.

The extent of division and disunity in the body of Christ today is legendary. We score very low on Jesus's scale of love. Everyone is concerned about his own problems. Very few people are reaching out to society with the kingdom message, to spread the kingdom of God using their resources in their sphere of influence and take it to remote parts of the world.

The Bible is so easy to understand. We often complicate things. "They shared everything" is a phrase strong enough to bring revival and revolution to the body of Christ, were we to implement it. They shared their money, clothing, houses, and food. God is calling us back to embrace true acts of love, a dimension of love that meets the standard laid out in 1 Corinthians 13.

The first church demonstrated in clear terms most of the attributes and principles identified by Jesus in the preceding sections. The key words here are "ownership" and "distribution." These are the two most critical concepts robbing today's church of influence. We are foolish about ownership and greedy about sharing. Everything we own was given to us. No man can receive anything, except it is given to him from above! Everything you and I own belongs to God. We are only stewards of heaven's resources and will one day give account of them.

There are four categories of people in today's church. They are shown in the chart below.

Ownership/ Distribution	I will distribute it	I won't distribute it
I own it	True love (partial impact on earth; partial rewards in heaven)	No love (selfish lifestyle, zero impact on earth, and no eternal reward in heaven)
We own it	True love (life of impact culminating in enormous eternal rewards)	Life of deception and religious bigotry (no impact on earth and no eternal reward in heaven)

I recommend that we all come to a stage in life where we see what God has given us as joint resources and utilize them wisely to meet the needs of humanity. I'm not recommending that we waste our resources or that we become Father Christmas, sharing money and materials to everybody we meet on the road. It's a state of the heart, a heart that feels the pain of others and isn't restricted by anything, but by God in meeting the needs of others as many times as necessary. That is the kind of person I trust God that I will ultimately become!

Someone might read this and interpret me wrongly. I don't mean that you begin to distribute and waste your resources indiscriminately. Please don't do so. You must be very wise in spending money. You must invest and make more than you presently have. But whatever you have must not have you. You must be willing to help others with your finances and resources as much as God helps you.

THE CASE OF ANANIAS AND SAPPHIRA

Another instance that perfectly revealed the state of the heart and attitude of the first church regarding finances and resources is the one in Acts 4:34–37. This account is different from the Ananias and Sapphira case study we will examine in more detail later on.

Neither was there any among them that lacked: for as many as were possessors of lands or houses sold them, and brought the prices of the things that were sold, and laid them down at the apostles' feet: and distribution was made unto every man according as he had need. And Joses, who by the apostles was surnamed Barnabas, (which is, being interpreted, The son of consolation,) a Levite, and of the country of Cyprus, having land, sold it, and brought the money, and laid it at the apostles' feet. (Acts 4:34–37)

From the above, we can see a number of important lessons for today's church. Can you imagine this statement? None of them lacked! What a terrible indictment of today's church. How many lacking people are in our churches and in society at large? If none lacked, it means they didn't lack. Can you imagine a church in America where out of thirty-five thousand members, none lacked? That sounds impossible.

But it is perfectly possible. The apostles so coordinated their welfare systems that everybody was well taken care of in every area of need. This is what church is all about: becoming and behaving like Jesus, looking for anyone with any kind of need in any area of life and meeting it in love.

The first sentence in the above is highly contestable, and many will use it as an excuse not to believe this entire section of the Bible. If all those who had houses and lands sold them, it means not everyone had houses and lands. It means that there were classes in the early church. Not everyone was rich. Yet the Bible states that they sold all their houses and lands and brought the funds to the apostles. Now, I'm not asking Christians to go about selling their houses and lands, but we've got to understand the context in which this scripture was written. These were the early days of the church. They were just getting an identity in the world. They were just forming a base. They were just building a system. They needed money for so many things.

They needed to develop structures, form committees, establish departments, and create a management and leadership structure. If all this was needed and some had assets that could be turned to money, while others didn't, then their new identity made it normal for them to dispose of those assets to meet the need at hand. The issue here is that the members of this early church and its leaders were so close to one another that the members trusted the early apostles to manage the proceeds of these sales very efficiently. If they didn't trust them, would they have brought all the funds to their feet? If you're pastor reading this, do your church members trust you with their money? Have you turned your church members into a cash machine that you withdraw from to meet your daily needs?

There is a particular church in the U.S. pastored by an African man. My wife is a friend of a church member who once complained enormously that the pastor milks the church dry. The pastor would stand on the altar and announce the names of the people who hadn't paid their tithes. He would tell the church the kind of shoes and designer clothes he liked and mandate them to buy the exact specification. Do you think these church members would sell their houses and bring the funds to the pastor's feet?

All over America and Africa, abuse of church funds has become the norm. Some weeks back, members of a popular Pentecostal church in Nigeria went on a public protest, accusing the leadership of their church of massive fraud. This protest was captured in one of Nigeria's newspapers. I was sad and ashamed! The name of Christ was dragged in the mud. Yet we are going about preaching to unbelievers to come to Christ!

THE APOSTLES WERE TRUSTWORTHY

In Acts 4:35, the term *"laid them down at the apostles' feet"* connotes a strikingly positive attribute about these members: humility. Can you lay something down at a man's feet without bending down? So folks who had houses could sell them, bend down at the apostles' feet, and turn back to remain members of the same fold. Many people in our generation with houses and lands wouldn't even sell their gardens, let alone bend down to give funds to a pastor.

The act of bending is an act of humility. In fact, it suggests that these members remained their natural self even after giving to the church. They didn't become untouchable sacred cows. In today's church, any man who gives gifts of such magnitude to God will seek to be seated in prominent sections of the church. Their pastors will not correct them again. They are sponsors of God's work and must not be disrespected! This is where we have found ourselves as members of this glorious church. No wonder we've become ineffective in so many ways.

Ananias and Sapphira were the bad eggs of the early church, but in the present-age they would get away with what they did. John MacArthur, Senior Pastor of Grace-to-You Church in California, describes Ananias and Sapphira's case like this: "They wanted to gain spiritual esteem and some cash along with it."[5]

This couple behaved the same way you and I have behaved in the past. But the Holy Spirit was setting a standard with the early church and wouldn't permit them to get away with it. The punishment was severe because they lied to the Holy Spirit and Jesus had said that sin against the Holy Spirit was not forgivable. The late Kenneth E. Hagin

---

[5] John MacArthur, *Ashamed of the Gospel: When the Church Becomes Like the World* (Wheaton, IL: Crossway Books, 2010), 70.

describes the sin against the Holy Spirit as the sin unto death that the Apostle John describes in 1 John 5:16:

If any man see his brother sin a sin which is not unto death, he shall ask, and he shall give him life for them that sin not unto death. There is a sin unto death: I do not say that he shall pray for it.

Something struck me in the above story. It seems like the apostles didn't care about money at the expense of living right. They weren't moved at the financial donations from Ananias and Sapphira. They were more concerned about their level of integrity, honesty, and truth. Living a life of lie, even when you're a major giver in the church, wasn't tolerated.

Can we relate to this in our present-day church? A man stole huge funds in a country in Africa and donated part of the funds to a popular church in the same country. The pastor didn't question the source of the funds, but accepted them. Months later, the fraud was detected and the man confessed that he had given an amount to the popular church. The police approached the church and they didn't deny it, but they refused to release the funds, claiming that they had been given to God! Unbelievable! You think God would accept such offering? Never. You cannot steal money and give it to God. It is unacceptable and an abomination. God desires your obedience more than your sacrifice.

Saul wanted to test this principle, but he paid for it with his throne and life. God doesn't place money above obedience. Obedience to God is a far greater premium in God's sight than all the money in the vaults of America. Oh how I wish our pastors would begin to verify the sources of funds paid into our church accounts. On that day, our influence in the world will soar. The world doesn't respect our messages the same way they respect our behaviour and lifestyle.

THE APOSTLE'S ATTITUDE TO MERCHANDISING THE ANOINTING

Another account of the early church's attitude toward finances is found in the story of Simon the Sorcerer in Acts 8:18–24:

And when Simon saw that through laying on of the apostles' hands the Holy Ghost was given, he offered them money, saying, Give me also this power, that on whomsoever I lay hands, he may receive the Holy Ghost.

But Peter said unto him, Thy money perish with thee, because thou hast thought that the gift of God may be purchased with money. Thou hast neither part nor lot in this matter: for thy heart is not right in the sight of God. Repent therefore of this thy wickedness, and pray God, if perhaps the thought of thine heart may be forgiven thee. For I perceive that thou art in the gall of bitterness, and in the bond of iniquity.

Then answered Simon, and said, Pray ye to the Lord for me, that none of these things which ye have spoken come upon me. (Acts 8:18–24).

VERY SCARY DETAILS!

There is a modern-day version of the above story. Many preachers now merchandise the anointing. What was Peter's response to Simon's request? Your money perishes with you! This is one of the worst judgments any man on earth could receive. When a man's money perishes with the man, we are talking about the memory of a man vanishing away. We are talking about a state of total annihilation. I'm happy that this incident occurred in the New Testament and cannot be wished away as being irrelevant to to-day's church. Come to think of it, Simon must have thought he was deal-ing with a powerless and docile church. He never expected such a swift judgement. Maybe he didn't remember the story of Ananias and Sapphira.

Anytime you want to trade finances for God's free gift, you stand the risk of incurring divine judgement. Many accounts have been told of men and women in Scripture who at one point or another attempted to trade their money for a desire. They either had the money and the desired gift was held by someone else, or they had the gift and someone else had the money. In either case, there were two parties involved in the exchange. Esau and Jacob are examples. So are Judas and the high priest.

John MacArthur gave an amazing account of Judas. According to MacArthur, Judas's story represents the world's worst account of lost opportunity! He sold the master for thirty pieces of silver. He wanted to exchange money with something of value, and he actually exchanged his place in the kingdom. How much are you worth? Can you be bought? Do you behave like Esau, who sold his birthright for a morsel of meat?

There are a lot of lessons for us to learn from the above passage. The apostles never endorsed any form of transactionary activity in the church. No amount of money could be exchanged for the anointing. Freely we have received, freely we must give; that was the state of their heart.

Where have we got things wrong in this present generation? The early church treasured relationship with God as a price for anything above financial inducement. I once read an account of the damage and cracks in the prosperity message. Pastor Israel Phiri presented the ten signs of a prosperity gospel that can eventually make a man poor. I love his account.

1. When it dominates the pulpit at the expense of Christocentric preaching.
2. When it is used as a big stick to keep you in line.
3. When money is a ticket for promotion or preferential treatment in ministry.
4. When it creates a keeping-up-with-the-Joneses spirit.
5. When it has no financial strategy beyond "just give."
6. When it creates a "man of God" dependency.
7. When it has an "If you leave me, you lose your blessing" clause.
8. When it never talks about education.
9. When it has a freebies mentality.
10. When it has a narrow definition of prosperity.[6]

A lot of terrible things are going on in different churches around the world, all in the name of financial empowerment. Pastors come on TBN

---

[6] Israel Phiri, *Impact Leaders Church*, "10 Signs of a Prosperity Gospel that Actually Makes You Poor." January 7, 2016 (http://impactleaderschurch.org/10-signs-of-a-prosperity-gospel-that-actually-makes-you-poor/).

and Daystar and ask people to sow seeds to connect with the anointing! That is totally wrong and sinful against God. I believe in sowing seeds. I have sowed to many ministries. I tell my wife, "Why don't they come out straight and raise an offering rather than mocking the name of Christ?" You cannot purchase any gift of the Holy Spirit by giving to the carrier of the gift. You can give material things to a carrier of a gift, and can receive material blessings from God, but you cannot sow to a healing evangelist to connect with the healing anointing so you too can raise the dead. If that happens, something else has been transferred to you which is not from God.

In the 1990s, a popular televangelist in Nigeria was accused of operating with occultic powers. This generated an enormous crisis in the body of Christ in Nigeria. One of my mentors loved this man (it is good to show love to anyone regardless of their faults) and never believed he was occultic. We argued about it many times and I rested my case since he couldn't be convinced otherwise. In 2008, I visited the same man of God and noticed that he had removed all the books of this televangelist from his library. I was puzzled and asked him why. He laughed and told me that he had disconnected from him. My inquisitive nature came to the fore and I queried him further.

He told me that a friend of his who pastored a church in a remote part of Nigeria got an invitation to attend a ministers' vigil, and he decided to honour the meeting. Upon getting to the venue, he discovered that they had to take a canoe to the actual place. In other words, they had to cross the waters. He was a bit puzzled, but decided to continue with the journey. As soon as he arrived at the venue of the meeting, to his surprise he saw the popular televangelist who had been accused of occultic affiliations in the 1990s. They were all given a form to fill out as part of the registration process, and a clause in the form mandated them never to disclose whatever happened in the meeting to third parties. The evangelist proceeded to minister powerfully and they served communion.

On getting back to his church the following Sunday, this man broke into the realm of the miraculous. All kinds of miracles began to happen. He was afraid and cried out to my friend on the phone that he was leaving town. This confirmed to my friend that he must have been initiated into a covenant by the communion served at the meeting and empowered satanically to perform miracles, signs, and wonders.

This is the reason that my friend decided to disconnect from the televangelist.

Strange story? Indeed. While it can be difficult to believe or understand if you're not familiar with these types of spirits, many spiritual practices are happening in Africa that affect the strength of their churches.

I was stunned by the above story and pondered on it for many years. The televangelist in question is extremely wealthy and has been introducing all manner of doctrines in his church since that time. Members contribute money towards his birthday every year. Every New Year's Eve celebration, he charges a gate fee to enter his church. All kinds of things have been reported about this man. We are now left with nothing except to continue praying for him that God would arrest him before it becomes too late.

Some months back, I was watching a minister of God on Daystar TV, a man whom I greatly respect. He brought another pastor I respect to his show and the guest pastor taught about the benefit of walking with God intimately in the end times. My ears pricked up because I easily fall in love with any message related to walking closely with God. If you want to catch my attention quickly, teach or preach on walking with God or hearing from God.

After hearing this very powerful message, I was blessed. I longed for more.

Then this pastor messed everything up. He told the viewers that if they wanted to walk closely with God and connect with Him in deep intimacy, they must sow a seed of closeness to God. I nearly fell off my seat. If a pastor could do this on a live program, what does he do in his own church? Such practices are evil and satanic. What is their end product? Destruction!

You cannot pay for any spiritual gift. It was freely given to you by God. You must freely give it to others. The only price to be paid is patience, prayer, fasting, longing, and panting after God.

There is a very popular church in Nigeria, and I am privy to the activities of its pastors. Many of them bribe their way to securing postings to what they call "juicy locations." This means that when a pastor is sent to lead a congregation in remote parts of the city where not many rich people live, the church's finances will be weak. On the other hand, when pastors are posted to serve in locations with many rich people, the chances of filling the church are much higher. Such pastors trade their destiny for financial opportunity. Atrocities begin to occur as pastors merchandize the anointing.

I have seen several cases of adultery, embezzlement, pride, and arrogance from such pastors. Is this how to advance the kingdom of God in our generation? If such a pastor dies in his sin, his ultimate destination is hell. There is no controversy around that. However, not every pastor trades money for the anointing. There are many incredible preachers in Nigeria, America, the UK, and in other parts of the world. They love God and live what they preach.

My ultimate focus in this book is to expose the errors in the use of finances in the twenty-first-century church. I also want to examine the sources of finances at the disposal of today's church to see if they comply with the standards laid out by God in the scriptures.

In this chapter, we have identified the financial practices of the early church. We have also identified the church's attitude about money, including the sources of their finances. These are the principles of the kingdom we must emulate if we are to behave like Jesus and extend the influence of the kingdom of God to our world.

SUMMARY OF CHAPTER TWO

1. Almsgiving is a kingdom practice endorsed by Jesus Himself.
2. There is no reference to giving alms only to Christians. Jesus used the word "men," and this refers to giving alms to every category of humans as long as there is a need for it.
3. For almsgiving, it is not a matter of if, but when. As believers, we must be involved in charities.
4. Almsgiving or charitable causes must not be done to attract undue attention from men. As much as is possible, we must do it as a private kingdom service to God.
5. God rewards charitable practices.

6. You must not worry about the lack of money or the lack of any other resource.

7. You must not acquire money or resources for the sole purpose of storing them up, but instead acquire it for the purpose of extending God's kingdom on earth to all categories of people, regardless of their religion.

8. A preacher of the gospel or a Christian brother or sister must not be overwhelmed by future needs that destroy their capacity to meet present needs. Simply put, Christians must focus on solving money problems from the present to the future, not from the future to the present.

9. No financial need, regardless how big and important, is permitted to make a Christian live in worry. You must not worry about money!

10. No preacher of the gospel or Christian must merchandize the anointing and power of God.

11. No preacher of the gospel or Christian must be motivated by the love for financial reward as a precondition for offering spiritual assistance to anybody. In other words, no preacher is permitted to request financial reward prior to offering spiritual assistance.

12. No one called by God into the ministry of the gospel can make the availability of financial resources the precondition for answering and running with the call.

13. Since there must be a purse, it is certain that God will provide the financial resources to fill up the purse after the call has been answered.

14. Jesus emphasized compassion for people above their lack of financial resources.

15. Jesus emphasized the solution to the need more than the source of the solution.

16. Rather than merchandizing the anointing to collect from people, Jesus showed that the opposite must be done. We must use the anointing to create solutions to the problems of people.

17. The early church was very sensitive to the needs of their members. Their approach was "If I have it, we all use it."

18. The early church never condoned unrighteousness in the life of givers. Regardless of how much you're giving, if your life is not right with God, your money is not acceptable to God.

19. Leaders who are trusted by followers attract financial donations more easily than those who cannot be trusted.

20. Members of the early church bent down to give. Bending is an act of humility. It means that in spite of one's financial standing, one is still humble in God's house.

21. You cannot give any amount of money to buy the power of God. Such requests are never granted by God, and in most cases they attract swift divine judgement.

CHAPTER THREE

MUST CHRISTIANS BE FINANCIALLY WEALTHY?

Beloved, I wish above all things that thou mayest prosper and be in health, even as thy soul prospereth. (3 John 1:2)

Before the end of this year, you will become a billionaire! Before the end of this year, you will hit your millions! I can hear my readers gently whispering "Amen." Maybe some are as radical as I am. They jump up and *scream* "Amen!"

These are now the most sought-after prayers among believers in our churches. They have the capacity to draw the largest crowd to any program. I need money, too. I'm not condemning it. I want to use finances to extend God's kingdom on earth. I need money to pay my bills and give my family (and society at large) the best of life.

But may I shock all of you? Your ultimate purpose in life is not to be rich. Wealth and riches are not the purpose for living. They are simply tools for achieving purpose. Or better put, they are means to an end, not the end by themselves. A leading pastor in the U.S. who has blessed me so much once said, "Your value is not determined by your valuables" and "Your self-worth is different from your net worth."

Many Christians have been held in bondage by the spirit of mammon, not knowing the principles of God's word on how to acquire, invest, and sustain money. The majority don't even know the purpose of money. Some see it as something to spend. Some see it as a tool for oppressing others. Others who are wise know that money can actually develop wings and fly away, so it must be invested.

> MONEY DOESN'T GRAVITATE TOWARDS PEOPLE WITH GOOD HEARTS, BUT TOWARDS PEOPLE WITH WISDOM— PEOPLE WHO HAVE THE WISDOM OF GOD FOR MAKING MONEY IN RIGHTEOUS WAYS, INCREASING IT IN CREDIBLE WAYS, AND USING IT IN KINGDOM WAYS.
>
> —*Pastor Sunday Adelaja*

One of my mentors, Pastor Sunday Adelaja in the Ukraine, once carried out a survey among members of his church. He asked them what they would do if they were to be given one million dollars. One person said he would pray and ask God to tell him what to spend it on. Pastor Sunday replied that he would never see the money, because he wasn't prepared for it. Someone else said he would donate to charities. Pastor Sunday said this was foolish, since money that isn't invested must not be immediately donated, as it would run out. He reiterated to his church members that although they had a good heart, unfortunately money doesn't gravitate towards people with good hearts, but towards people with wisdom—people who have the wisdom of God for making money in righteous ways, increasing it in credible ways, and using it in kingdom ways.

3 John 1:2 is one of the most abused scriptures in the bible. I wrote about this in great detail in another of my books, *Building and Sustaining a Life of Wisdom*. There are three areas of prosperity the Bible refers to: physical prosperity, intellectual prosperity, and spiritual prosperity. We often confuse wealth with prosperity. They are totally different. Prosperity is the umbrella under which wealth resides. A man can be wealthy, yet not prosperous. A man with a billion dollars who is terribly sick with cancer and who is not born again is not prosperous in God's eyes. Yes, he is wealthy, and might even be intellectually prosperous, but he is certainly not spiritually and physically prosperous. When your body is dying on the sickbed, you are not physically prosperous. When you're not born again, and upon dying your destination is hell, you are not spiritually prosperous. So what we call wealth is completely different from the generic term "prosperity." The apostle John makes this

very clear. God doesn't want partial prosperity. In other words, being a billionaire without Christ is useless and valueless in God's eyes.

If you don't combine the three areas of prosperity, don't even say you are prosperous. A lot of people with fat bank accounts on earth and very poor people in heaven.

Many pastors now teach that God's ultimate goal is for Christians to become wealthy. This is a wrong theology and very offensive to God. Rather than teaching Christians to be totally prosperous in all three areas—spiritual, intellectual, and physical—the emphasis is on maintaining fat bank accounts. Brothers and sisters, your bank account on earth might be fat, but if your account of kingdom service in heaven isn't fat, you are a very poor man. Your destination might be hell, unless you come to the saving grace of Jesus.

Spiritual prosperity will forever be superior to intellectual or physical prosperity. God wishes above all things that you prosper in the spirit (become born again and grow to maturity as a Christian), prosper intellectually (become very intelligent, skilful, and effective in your calling and purpose in life), and prosper physically (have abundance and sufficiency to fulfill your God-given purpose).

Therefore, your ultimate desire as a Christian should not be the pursuit of wealth (physical prosperity) alone, but rather spiritual prosperity, the driver of wealth. The degree to which you seek the expansion of God's kingdom through spiritual growth and investment in God will determine the extent of the power for wealth God releases in you.

A lot of terrible things are happening in many churches around the world. Many pastors have corrupted God's word, teaching believers the exact opposite of what God wants them to learn. I don't hate the gospel of prosperity, and I disagree that it's entirely satanic, as some of my brothers in Christ assume. But I also disagree with the notion that every Christian must pursue wealth and riches, at the expense of kingdom pursuit. The Bible is clear. You and I must seek *first* the kingdom of God, before any other pursuit.

If the kingdom is paramount to God, why are His servants teaching men to seek wealth and money? Your number one pursuit in life must be the kingdom of God (spiritual prosperity) and find ways to expand it through the fulfillment of your purpose. Don't allow your pastor to deceive and confuse you. Make God's word, not your pastor, your number one standard.

In my opinion, the only group of people who qualifies for major financial supply from God are those who are expanding God's kingdom through their purpose. Let's say you have been raised by God as a medical doctor and given the mandate to care for men and women. You have discovered this calling and have remained committed to it. You are born again and walk with God in sincerity to see Him use you to care for millions around the world. If this is you, you cannot escape major financial empowerment. Of course, you must be a man of vision, interested in providing medical care to millions. Such a man will certainly command major financial abundance if he remains committed to his vision.

Many of us don't even know what the definition of vision is. You're living for yourself. You've disconnected from your purpose in life. You do whatever you want and you're crying to God for financial empowerment. To do what with it? You are not kingdom-minded and don't qualify for God's financial empowerment.

Of course, Satan also empowers people financially. No one collects money from Satan and doesn't regret it. For it is the blessing of God that makes us rich and adds no sorrow (Proverbs 10:22).

For many years, I was confused as to why I gave to God and never became rich. I asked questions of those who had gone ahead of me. I always gave in church programs when offerings were collected. I responded to every TV evangelist calling for special offerings. I sowed like a madman. Yet I got nothing back.

I questioned God. I questioned many men of God. None of them provided me the right answers. Why would I be giving so much and not get any return as promised? I wanted to become wealthy, as had been prophesied by a pastor. Of course, as a minister of the gospel myself, I have taught people the same sets of principles, often ignoring the vital ingredients that are necessary to commit God to fulfilling His word in people's lives. Then came a season in my life when I jumped into the mainstream of God's purpose and I began to write books and sell them. My books went all over the world. I paid for all publishing costs and bore all the pains. I simply forgot about my questions about why God hadn't made me wealthy and forged ahead with my calling.

One day, I was getting my hair cut at a barber's shop in Toronto, Canada, when the Lord spoke to me to approach a leading man of God for something. I hesitated because I had no access to this man. With the help of the Holy Spirit, I sent a Facebook message to this great apostle, thinking he wouldn't even reply. He replied and requested that I help him write a book at a price. I was stunned. Of all the people in the world? I was to write a book for this great man of God? I would write the book and he would put his name on it and also acknowledge me in the book. I couldn't believe it. He requested to pay me, but I declined. I told him that I wanted grace, not money. God had worked on me to a point where a man who had once been clamouring for a harvest declined it when it was given. I said, "No, sir. Just bless me and I will do this work without taking a dime from you."

> STOP RUNNING AFTER WEALTH. RUN AFTER PURPOSE. PURPOSE FULFILLMENT WILL BRING WEALTH!

I finished the book project, and on the day I thanked him for giving me the opportunity, the great man of God told me he would reward me by connecting me with an enormous opportunity for wealth. It was like I couldn't hear him, so I recorded his voice on my phone to listen to the conversation again later. He simply connected me to the world's greatest source of wealth, and that was it! Wealth didn't come while I was busy giving, and possibly throwing away, money; it came when I discovered God's purpose for my life, committed myself to it, and began to extend God's kingdom.

How instructive is this story? Stop running after wealth. Run after purpose. Purpose fulfillment will bring wealth!

Must Christians be financially wealthy? A very important question. Yes, those who have discovered God's purpose for their lives and are living it to the extent that the kingdom of God is being expanded and impacted on earth have more than enough provisions to fulfill their vision. Those who don't even know God's purpose for their lives and are merely living for themselves don't qualify for any major provisions from God.

However, there are still many earthly laws that are capable of attracting finances and wealth into the lives of believers or unbelievers. My Bible teaches that our God gives the power to get wealth (Deuteronomy 8:18). The ultimate power for wealth is in the hands of God. All earthly laws and principles that men operate to get wealth flow from God's ultimate wisdom and power. Since He created every resource on earth, regardless of the principles taught in the world, God is still the overall owner of the power for wealth, just as Satan possesses the power for wealth. Satan gives a lot of people wealth. I therefore recognize the need for operating the laws and principles of money that are earthly specific. However, I defer the ultimate power for sustainable wealth to God.

Other human laws and principles can make men wealthy, but it's not sustainable. Empires can collapse. Businesses can fail. Stock prices can crash, and believe me, oil prices can fall. If your wealth is solely based on the principles and wisdom of the world, as the world collapses, you will collapse with it.

Robert Kyosaki, author of the famous book *Rich Dad, Poor Dad*, taught many people about the laws of money and made a lot of money himself—but he has just been declared bankrupt! Are you surprised? I'm not rejoicing at his downfall, and neither am I mocking him. I want him back on his feet to continue to bless the world. But is it an accident that he crashed? His money principles are amazing and have helped many people, but they cannot sustain success. He actually left God out of his principles and based his principles solely on human logic and human wisdom. Human wisdom and logic can only take a man as far as his wisdom and logic. They never last forever. God's wisdom lasts forever, and every other thing connected to this wisdom lasts forever. Get my book *Building and Sustaining a Life of Wisdom* and you will be mightily blessed by it.

For the believer, your ultimate goal is total prosperity, not financial prosperity alone. In my opinion, and based on God's word, all Christians must be totally prosperous—prosperous in their spirits, prosperous in their minds, and prosperous in their bodies.

SUMMARY OF CHAPTER THREE

1. Your ultimate purpose in life is not to become financially wealthy, but to discover your purpose, fulfill it, and extend God's kingdom on earth.
2. Money flows towards people who have the wisdom of God for making it in righteous ways, increasing it in credible ways, and using it in kingdom ways.
3. You can be wealthy on earth and still be poor in heaven. Spiritual prosperity is forever superior to physical prosperity (wealth).
4. Total prosperity (spiritual, intellectual, and physical) is God's number one priority for your life.
5. Stop running after wealth. Run after purpose. Purpose fulfillment will bring wealth!
6. The degree to which you extend God's kingdom on earth through your discovery and commitment to His purpose for your life is the degree to which your life will command financial resources and other needed provisions.
7. As a pastor, you shouldn't lead your sheep in the hot pursuit for wealth at the expense of the kingdom. Extending the kingdom of God is the heart cry of God and should be the number one focus of every Christian.
8. You can, of course, become wealthy by simply operating the laws and principles of money on earth. You don't have to be a Christian to make money. But if your financial prosperity doesn't have God at the centre, it's not sustainable. You should see God as the centre of every resource and provision in this world and link your prosperity to Him.

CHAPTER FOUR

EMPIRE BUILDERS OR
ARK BUILDERS?

Make thee an ark of gopher wood; rooms shalt thou make in the ark, and shalt pitch it within and without with pitch… And of every living thing of all flesh, two of every sort shalt thou bring into the ark, to keep them alive with thee; they shall be male and female.
(Genesis 6:14, 19)

The quest for money at all costs has completely blinded many Christians to the difference between arks and empires. I explained the differences between these two words in one of my books, *The Days of Noah*, a must-read for any Christian who places value on the end times. In it, I wrote,

> EMPIRES ARE RAISED TO SERVE THE OWNERS. ARKS ARE RAISED TO SERVE NOT JUST THE OWNERS, BUT ALL HUMANITY. EMPIRES DRIVE SELFISHNESS. ARKS DRIVE GENEROSITY.

There is a difference between empires and arks. God spoke to Noah to make himself an ark. That ark was to serve as a security and protection against the coming holocaust. That ark was supposed to serve Noah's family and the families of every known species of animal. God prepared Noah for posterity, and not for prosperity, a major difference between arks and empires. Empires are raised to serve the owners. Arks are raised to serve not just the owners, but all humanity. Empires drive selfishness. Arks drive generosity. Most men and women who have been empowered financially by God in this generation fall into the categories of ark builders or empire builders.

If you look at the entire world, the majority of nations that are at war with other nations are empire builders. This is one of the major attributes of the days of Noah. Men and women, whether inside or outside the church, will invest massively in building their empires to satisfy their lust for relevance and prominence. There are empire builders in the business world. There are empire builders in the academic world. There are empire builders in the church. Many pastors have been trapped into the web of empire building. They simply accumulate wealth and affluence to prepare abundance for their children when they pass on. The Bible has something to say about the days we are living in.

This know also, that in the last days perilous times shall come. For men shall be lovers of their own selves, covetous, boasters, proud, blasphemers, disobedient to parents, unthankful, unholy... *(2 Timothy 3:1–2)*

Men who love themselves more than others belong to the category of people we're talking about in this section. These are the empire builders.

Can you be honest with yourself? Are you building arks or building empires? Do you love yourself more than you love others? Yes, the Bible tells us that we must love our neighbours as much as we love ourselves, but not loving ourselves more than our neighbours. If Jesus loved himself more than the world, will you and I be saved? See what Jesus did for you and me in raising an ark of salvation for us.

But God commendeth his love toward us, in that, while we were yet sinners, Christ died for us. *(Romans 5:8)*

It is love that drives people to raise arks of safety, not just for themselves, but to preserve posterity for others. What efforts are you putting into the development of your career and business as a Christian to protect future generations? Do you invest in charitable causes? Do you support the education of orphans and other less privileged groups? Are you only passionate about

IT IS LOVE THAT DRIVES PEOPLE TO RAISE ARKS OF SAFETY, NOT JUST FOR THEMSELVES, BUT TO PRESERVE POSTERITY FOR OTHERS.

the growth and success of your children, even when you know you are financially prosperous enough to support one hundred other less privileged children?

Ark builders are characterized by practices and activities that are geared towards building future generations. Empires don't stand the test of storms, but fortunately arks do. All those who owned empires during the time of Noah lost them to the holocaust. Only Noah's ark stood the test of the holocaust.

Nothing in this world lasts forever. Posterity is forever superior to prosperity. We are living in the days of Noah. These are the days of empire builders. Dare to be an ark builder and you are sure to stand the test of time as we move towards the most critical moment in history.

The vast majority of men and women in the kingdom of God who have been entrusted with wealth are building empires. Of course, many others are building arks. The ultimate purpose of every resource God gave Noah was not just to preserve the memory of his family, but to secure the future of other generations of animals and every other species.

There is now a widespread epidemic of empire builders among ministers of the gospel in today's church. All over the world, you see this trend. Of course, there is nothing wrong with ministers of the gospel investing in businesses if God has led them to do that and they are kingdom-minded. However, for the most part, the opposite is the case. Many preachers publicly claim that they are kingdom minded, but their actions and practices prove otherwise.

There is now an epidemic of university projects among preachers in Nigeria. God has given every preacher the vision to start a university! Perish the thought. Truly, there must be some people whom God has led to do this. But I don't believe God has led everybody to do the same thing. Why would God give every preacher the same vision? Of all the troubles facing our world, will only university projects dominate God's attention? No. It is mere ambition, a passion to build an empire that will outlast the minister.

The consequence of this is pressure being placed on church members to sow, sow, and sow towards these projects, even to the point of bleeding. It is a sin to build empires upon the sweat of givers. If you are a preacher and you see nothing wrong in this, you're standing on the threshold of severe eternal judgment from God. Everything may seem right here on earth, but one day you will stand before the one who cannot be deceived—the God of the whole universe who knows the heart of men and cannot be unjust.

In America, there is also an epidemic of empire builders. Most of the big men of God service their relationships with political leaders and fail to speak the truth, all in the name of being politically correct. Ask them any question about gay and lesbianism and they would reply with a question. They don't want to offend the gays and lesbians in their churches. True wealth from God empowers a man to do more for God: to build arks of safety for others, to build schools and orphanages for the downtrodden, and to feed millions of children in war-ravaged countries. The list is endless.

Ark builders are becoming scarce. Empire builders are plentiful. Where do you belong? Pastors are building up wealth for their unborn children to the point of diverting church funds. It is not a sin to make money; it is a sin to exploit others to make money.

And he spake a parable unto them, saying, The ground of a certain rich man brought forth plentifully: and he thought within himself, saying, What shall I do, because I have no room where to bestow my fruits? And he said, This will I do: I will pull down my barns, and build greater; and there will I bestow all my fruits and my goods. And I will say to my soul, Soul, thou hast much goods laid up for many years; take thine ease, eat, drink, and be merry. But God said unto him, Thou fool, this night thy soul shall be required of thee: then whose shall those things be, which thou hast provided? So is he that layeth up treasure for himself, and is not rich toward God.
(Luke 12:16–21)

This story has been popular in the body of Christ for many centuries. These six verses contain deep revelations about the differences between empire builders and ark builders. Let's compare the differences.

EMPIRE BUILDERS	ARK BUILDERS
Empire builders have access to finances (resources) through personal investments.	Ark builders have access to finances (resources) through personal investments.
Empire builders spend time thinking about how to make more money and what to do for themselves with this money.	Ark builders may spend time thinking about how to make more money, but their minds are preoccupied with extending the kingdom of God on earth and impacting society with the money
Empire builders expand their influence on the support of others.	Ark builders expand their influence through themselves and their immediate families.
Empire builders never create the capacity for others to benefit from their money.	Ark builders create the capacity for others to benefit from their money.
Empire builders look for bigger and greater opportunities to increase their wealth, often piling it up for self-aggrandizement and personal ego.	Ark builders might look for bigger and greater opportunities to increase their wealth, but they look for opportunities to use this wealth for the benefit of mankind.
Empire builders rationalize their actions, often placing importance on their logic as justification for building wealth.	Ark builders are kingdom-minded in the quest to build wealth.
Empire builders are mostly concerned with pleasure (eating, drinking and merrymaking).	Ark builders are more concerned with solving problems than pleasure (eating, drinking, and merrymaking).
Empire builders are mostly concerned about the size of storage, not the size of distribution.	Ark builders are mostly concerned about the size of distribution, not the size of storage.

THE 80/20 RULE OF MONEY FOR THE CHURCH

The 80/20 principle has been applied in many organizational settings. It examines the proportion of resources or people or entities that contribute the least or greatest to a current phenomenon. For example, we can say that eighty percent of all staff members in an organization contribute a total of twenty percent of their income to a staff savings plan, or twenty percent of the staff contribute eighty percent of their income. I have found this principle to be relevant to the current topic. Many people who have enormous wealth in the body of Christ don't know how to coordinate the distribution of that wealth. Though some still give to many causes, the fraction of what they give isn't enough to make any significant impact on the problems confronting the world at large. Some have given twenty percent of their finances to charity, often keeping eighty percent to themselves and their families and ministries.

However, Jesus would never do that. He gave everything. I'm advocating a revolution among Christians such that those who have huge finances can commit and invest eighty percent of their wealth to extending God's kingdom on earth, in their spheres of influence. This is a hard saying and not many people can handle it. Am I saying we should give everything away and become poor again? I'm not advocating for wasteful and indiscriminate use of money. Every penny must be wisely invested. There are people whose twenty percent is still massively sufficient to sustain them and their generations. I'm speaking to people whom God has given access to massive wealth.

You cannot invest eighty percent of your excess wealth to the cause of the gospel and the kingdom of God on earth and not attract the favour and blessings of God. Didn't you read the story of the boy who gave Jesus his lunch? Do you think Jesus would have sent him away emptyhanded? Where do you think the twelve baskets were later sent to? I believe they were handed over to the parent of this boy. Your reward in heaven will be unthinkable. The result among the body of Christ if the rich among us flipped their distribution formula would turn the world upside down.

The story of John D. Rockefeller is amazing. History tells us that he gave God a ninety percent tithe and kept ten percent. Generations after him are still celebrating him today. Have you also read the news about Bill Gates and Mark Zuckerberg giving up major portions of their wealth out to charity? Most of these people aren't even born again, yet they're setting the pace for many of us to follow. We should be at the vanguard.

Some of us have been blessed by God to the point that our basic needs have been met. The excess of our finances are enormous and can change the world. These are the people I'm talking to. Of course, this is not a rule or a law. We should all give according to our faith and grace. I will, however, encourage us to grow in our giving and chase away the empire-building spirit and welcome the grace to be ark builders for God. By doing this, we truly become ambassadors for Jesus on earth. The kingdom of God will be further extended and expanded and we will lay up massive treasures in heaven where no thief can approach.

SUMMARY OF CHAPTER FOUR

1. Empires drive selfishness. Arks drive generosity. Arks are raised to serve not just the owners, but all humanity.
2. Your ultimate goal in life as a Christian and preacher is to become an ark builder for God.
3. It is love that drives people to raise arks of safety, not just for themselves, but for posterity's sake.
4. It is a sin to build empires with the sweat of givers. If you are a preacher and you see nothing wrong in this, you are standing on the threshold of severe eternal judgment from God.

CHAPTER FIVE

THE PURPOSE OF TITHES AND OFFERINGS
IN THE CHURCH

Bring ye all the tithes into the storehouse, that there may be meat in mine house, and prove me now herewith, saith the Lord of hosts, if I will not open you the windows of heaven, and pour you out a blessing, that there shall not be room enough to receive it. (Malachi 3:10)

The subject of tithes and offerings has remained a debate among Christians. Many scholars even criticize the principle of tithing. They argued that it doesn't apply to New Testament believers. I don't agree with these findings. I believe with every fibre of my being that tithes and offerings, or any other form of giving, are eternal principles ordained by God. It is the abuse of these principles that makes the subject a matter of debate.

Abraham was the first example of a tither (Genesis 14:20). We always claim the promises of Abraham. The Abrahamic covenant is an eternal covenant. God made this clear to Abraham. Consequently, tithing is ordained by God and applies to all New Testament believers. Look at the following scriptures:

And blessed be the most high God, which hath delivered thine enemies into thy hand. And he gave him tithes of all. (Genesis 14:20)

But he whose descent is not counted from them received tithes of Abraham, and blessed him that had the promises. (Hebrew 7:6)

But woe unto you, Pharisees! for ye tithe mint and rue and all manner of herbs, and pass over judgment and the love of God: these ought ye to have done, and not to leave the other undone. (Luke 11:42)

And here men that die receive tithes; but there he receiveth them, of whom it is witnessed that he liveth. And as I may so say, Levi also, who receiveth tithes, payed tithes in Abraham. (Hebrews 7:8–9)

Some have said that there is no New Testament reference to support tithing. Take a look at the above. Hebrews 7 clearly dispels that wrong notion. The writer of Hebrews makes it unambiguous that men receive tithes, and such tithes are received by God in heaven. The "he" in the first phrase refers to God, to whom tithes are paid as commanded in Malachi 3:10. I believe anyone in doubt of the authenticity of tithing should now be convinced.

My focus in this section is not about promoting or disproving the principle of tithing, but to shine the light of God's word on how tithes and offerings must be used to the glory of God.

Dr. Myles Munroe once wrote, in his book *In Pursuit of Purpose*, that when you don't know the purpose of a thing, abuse is inevitable.[7] I strongly believe that many pastors, including givers themselves, don't know the purpose of tithes and offerings. Consequently, they abuse the practice.

God instituted tithing in the Old Testament and made it clear how it must be used. Any other use outside of God's specifications would certainly attract consequences, for our God is not a respecter of persons, but of principles. In other words, whether or not you know God's standards about the use of tithes and offerings, you're not absolved of the consequences of the inappropriate use of tithes and offerings. Consider the following scripture:

And that servant, which knew his lord's will, and prepared not himself, neither did according to his will, shall be beaten with

---

[7] Dr. Myles Monroe, *In Pursuit of Purpose* (Shippensburg, PA: Destiny Image, 1992).

many stripes. But he that knew not, and did commit things worthy of stripes, shall be beaten with few stripes. For unto whomsoever much is given, of him shall be much required: and to whom men have committed much, of him they will ask the more.
(Luke 12:47–48)

There is a consequence for the wrong use of tithes and offerings. Pastors and general overseers, beware!

Tithes are symbols of covenants. Everyone who gives tithes to God is fulfilling his portion of the Abrahamic covenant. A covenant is a binding agreement between two or more parties. In this context, God is the covenantor. We are the covenantee. Abraham, Jacob, and the rest of the patriarchs who gave tithes to God did so as a covenant relationship with God. They all wanted God to do certain things for them while they paid their tithes. This is why the Holy Spirit through the prophet Malachi spoke the most direct instructions about tithing in the form of an agreement between two parties. Malachi 3:10, paraphrased, says, "You bring your tithe and I will do…"

Have you ever seen anyone break a covenant without any consequence? In the occultic world, covenants are bound by blood. Satan doesn't play games with his protégés. You break his covenant, you pay for it with your blood. Of course, we now live under grace. God isn't going to kill His children simply because they haven't paid their tithes. But know certainly that there is a consequence for every form of disobedience in God's word.

But what was the original purpose in the heart of God for the use of tithes and offerings. What is purpose in itself? I love Dr. Myles Munroe's definition. He says that purpose is the original intent behind the creation of a thing.[8]

So what was God's original intent about tithes?

Bring ye all the tithes into the storehouse, that there may be meat in mine house, and prove me now herewith, saith the Lord of hosts, if I will not open you the windows of heaven, and pour

---

[8] Ibid.

you out a blessing, that there shall not be room enough to receive it.
(Malachi 3:10, emphasis added)

Take a look at the emphasized phrase: *"Bring ye all the tithes into the storehouse, that there may be meat in mine house."* The New King James Version translates "meat" as "food". The Message Bible translates "meat" as "provisions". Most other versions use "food" as the direct interpretation for "meat".

So the original intent in the heart of God is to have food, or provision, in the storehouse.

Now, what does the word "storehouse" mean? The original Hebrew word for "storehouse" is *RCWA* and is translated into English as treasure, treasury, treasure house, or armoury. Simply put, the number one purpose of tithing is to provide resources for maintaining God's house. Since resources must be used up in the achievement of set objectives, tithes also must be used up by those appointed by God to manage His storehouse. Without any complicated interpretation, every storehouse or treasury house must have the following characteristics:

- There must be a store manager or treasury manager.
- There must be a form of security or control.
- There must be a two-way channel into the storehouse. Resources must go in and out.
- There must be some sets of activities and work to be carried out with these resources.

Are you a pastor? Can you relate with the above? Does your church have these characteristics? Several other scriptures point to the sacred nature and purpose of tithes. They describe those who must collect and administer tithes taken from people. Consider God's instructions:

Thus speak unto the Levites, and say unto them, When ye take of the children of Israel the tithes which I have given you from them for your inheritance, then ye shall offer up an heave offering of it for the Lord, even a tenth part of the tithe. (Numbers 18:26)

And the priest the son of Aaron shall be with the Levites, when the Levites take tithes: and the Levites shall bring up the tithe of the tithes unto the house of our God, to the chambers, into the treasure house. (Nehemiah 10:38)

It has now become easy to create a framework for understanding tithing in terms of its purpose, its source, its destination, and the people required by God to supervise it.

TITHES	CHARACTERISTICS
The source of tithes	Christians (believers). If you are not saved in Christ, you can't be paying tithes to God.
The purpose of tithes	To act as provision or resources in God's storehouses.
The users of tithes (administrators)	Levites (priests in God's house, who in our present dispensation are pastors and leaders of churches or any other Christian organization).
The ultimate destination of tithes	God (heaven).

We can now see clearly what God's word, the Bible, recommends about tithing. Of course, the four dimensions of tithing sometimes create confusion in the church. For example, must only Christians pay tithe? Can tithes be used for things other than provisions or resources in God's house? Are pastors or church leaders the only approved administrators of the tithes of the people? Are we sure tithes are truly ultimately recognized and accepted by God in heaven?

Most church leaders have misused tithes, while a vast majority even teach that once you tithe, all your problems are over. They fail to realize that tithing is not sufficient to make a man successful. They miss a vital element of tithing: the blessing.

If we must gain a robust understanding of the purpose of tithes and offerings in the church today, we need to understand the reaction of

God to faithful tithing. What does God do to people who tithe? When combined, all of these revelations are able to strengthen our conviction on the appropriate use of tithes. We will be able to do things that are pleasing to God.

THE REACTION OF GOD TO FAITHFUL TITHING

What happens to me if I pay my tithe faithfully? What happens if I don't? Does God really curse His children in the New Testament? Haven't we been redeemed from the curse of the law? There are many people who don't tithe yet are successful. Why are things the way they are? I thought about these many questions for many years, until the Lord began to reveal things to me.

> *Bring ye all the tithes into the storehouse, that there may be meat in mine house, and prove me now herewith, saith the Lord of hosts, if I will not open you the windows of heaven, and pour you out a blessing, that there shall not be room enough to receive it.* (Malachi 3:10).

> *And here men that die receive tithes; but there he receiveth them, of whom it is witnessed that he liveth.* (Hebrews 7:8)

We have established that God truly receives the tithes of men. When you pay tithes to your church or to wherever you consider your storehouse (where God has led you to be fed and nourished spiritually), you are actually paying it to God in obedience to His word. Look at Hebrews 7:8, above. The "he" in that scripture is God. God receives your tithes when you pay them to your church.

Now, we need to establish what truly represents a storehouse. Some people argue that they're not fed spiritually in their church, and consequently they send their tithes to another church. I'm not here to recommend the best church on earth to my wonderful readers. However, please note that God is the best selector of your place of worship. God actually appoints pastors for His sheep. If you can trust God with the responsibility of your place of worship, He will lead you to the right place. Regardless of what you experience in the place God leads you to, you don't have any spiritual right to change your church without God's leading. If you fall out of favour with your pastor, look for an opportunity to reconcile with him. You must learn to forgive and forget. Create room for reconciliation. However, in circumstances where a pastor doesn't walk in line with God's word or is perpetually living in sin, you have the right to pray and ask God to lead you on what to do. God could tell you to stay and continue to pray for that pastor. God could lead you to another church.

What I'm saying here is so important. It has cost many Christians the harvest for their tithes and offerings. Kenneth Copeland, in one of his books, supported this notion and emphasized the need for Christians to not throw their tithes and offerings everywhere. He argued that the majority of Christians have not been rewarded by God because their tithes and offerings went to the wrong place, a place that was not appointed by God to cater for their spiritual needs.

And I will give you pastors according to mine heart, which shall feed you with knowledge and understanding. (Jeremiah 3:15)

Simply put, the place that qualifies as your storehouse, into where your tithes must go, is the place God has appointed for you and led you to. Secondly, you must be certain and convinced with proofs that you are being fed with knowledge and understanding of God's word in that place. If you are experiencing the opposite, God might not have led you there. God is not the author of confusion. He knows the kind of food your destiny needs. He will not lead you to a place where you will be malnourished spiritually.

If you have been led to the right storehouse, your tithes and offerings must support God's work in that place. Of course, you can still give free will offerings to many other good causes, in any other storehouse outside of your present storehouse, but your secondary storehouse must not be nourished at the expense of your primary storehouse. You can't be sending your offerings to a church in Germany when your local church is in need, and your eyes are closed to that need.

WHEN YOU PAY YOUR TITHES, WHAT IS YOUR REWARD?

Malachi 3:10 is our anchor scripture. The Bible makes it clear that God will *"open you the windows of heaven, and pour you out a blessing, that there shall not be room enough to receive it."* God will open the windows of heaven. This means that the windows of heaven can be closed. Jesus experienced an open heaven right after His baptism at the River Jordan. What that statement means is extremely powerful. When the heaven over a man is closed, revelations and interactions from the throne room of God are terminated. You are simply in a state where you can't hear the voice of the Holy Spirit again, though He is still living inside you as a New Testament Christian. It is possible to grief the Holy Spirit. The New Testament says so.

> *And grieve not the holy Spirit of God, whereby ye are sealed unto the day of redemption.* (Ephesians 4:30)

When heaven is opened over your life, it is an indication of the free flow of communication with and information from the Holy Spirit. You can't miss it. Every exploit in the Kingdom of God is provoked by revelation, so if the source of revelation if corrupted or closed, you are far from those exploits. In other words, God is eternally committed to keeping the traffic of heaven in your life active if you are committed to obeying Him in the payment of your tithes.

Note that the Bible doesn't say God will pour down money or houses or cars. Most of us pay tithes and expect money to be given to us by God as rewards. God can bless you in return using any means. The word "blessing" in Hebrew means "empowered to prosper or succeed." Power is the ability to work or do something. In other words, you are empowered with supernatural ability to prosper or succeed when you pay your tithes. This ability could come in the form of a unique idea. It could come in the form of a unique insight or solution to a problem. In fact, it could come in the form of favour and grace. You can be so favoured by God that men will seek you out to help you. God can also send the right people across your path. We can't pin God down with what He should do in return for our faithfulness to tithing. He can reward us using any means.

And I will rebuke the devourer for your sakes, and he shall not destroy the fruits of your ground; neither shall your vine cast her fruit before the time in the field, saith the Lord of hosts. (Malachi 3:11)

Now wait a minute. Does that mean that when I'm faithful in the payment of my tithe, Satan will no longer attack me? Far from the truth. The devourer, Satan himself, will still attempt to destroy you. He will still attempt to destroy your harvest. God is saying that you will prevail over him. The matter of attempting to attack you is not the issue here, but the outcome of the attack.

Two major prophetic blessings emerge from the above scripture:
• Satan the devourer is not permitted to destroy the fruits of your ground.
• Satan the devourer is not permitted to abort the fruit of your body before the right time of delivery.

These are extremely powerful prophetic blessings. Note that Satan is not that concerned about your seeds or labour of planting the seeds. He can wait and allow you to sweat and labour to plant your seed. What he's after is the harvest. That is where the greatest pain lies. When a man has laboured and is right at the point of harvest, Satan loves to strike and destroy the harvest. No pain is greater than that. A lot of women raise children and struggle to send them to school. When the child is about to graduate and the parent is at the point of enjoying the fruit of her labour, Satan strikes the child with a terminal disease. That is his primary ministry. John 10:10 emphasizes his stealing, killing, and destruction.

Secondly, Satan loves to abort visions before they are ripe for manifestation. Are you carrying a great vision? Satan loves to terminate that vision before its time of fulfillment. That is his ministry. What God does when you obey Him and are faithful with tithing is to block Satan's access to inflicting the above two calamities on you. He has no authority to do it.

Your obedience to God in the payment of your tithes draws the hand of God to empower you to succeed. Now, empowerment for success is a relative concept. If you sleep all day, you will be empowered to fail. God's blessings always come upon the works of your hands. Idleness breeds failure and poverty. Regardless of how many years you have been faithful in paying your tithe, if you're not working, or you're working but are not diligent, your tithe will not yield any result. So many Christians pay tithes and still struggle and remain poor. You must strive to be excellent in all you do.

I explained this issue of excellence in detail in one of my books, *Building and Sustaining a Life of Wisdom*. The process of determining God's response to faithfulness in tithe payment is described as follows:

- You must prayerfully determine the right church to attend. That church is the storehouse where your tithes must be paid.
- That church must feed you with knowledge and understanding of God's word. No heresy is permitted. Otherwise you have the right to pray and ask God to lead you to change your church.
- When you faithfully pay your tithe, God commits to doing four things for you:
  — He will open the windows of heaven for you.
  — He will pour blessings down on you.
  — He will not allow Satan the devourer to destroy the fruits of your ground.
  — He will not allow Satan the devourer to abort the fruit of your body before the right time of delivery.

WHAT ABOUT OFFERINGS?
The same is true of living a life of giving. None of us can out-give God. You must be strongly committed to giving to the cause of charity and to the cause of advancing the spread of the gospel across the globe. The blessings are just too much to mention here. Millions of missionaries are going around the globe to spread the gospel. Your offerings can support their causes, and you can certainly be part of their reward in heaven.

Evangelist Reinhard Bonnke once shared the story of a man named Rudolph. This man lived in Germany and was best described as destitute in appearance. He looked poor, he stank, and was dirty. But whenever he attended Bonnke's meetings, he would demand to see the man of God after the service. The first time he did so, Bonnke didn't want to grant him any serious audience. But he was shocked when Rudolph dipped his hand inside his dirty clothes and brought out a stack of money running into tens of thousands of deutsche marks. He told the man of God to use it as his contribution towards the cause of the gospel in Africa. Bonnke was so stunned. Rudolph eventually emptied all his life savings, in the form of his pension from the German government, to support the spread of the gospel in Africa through Reinhard Bonnke. How fat do you think Rudolph's account is in heaven?

That is what it means to be a giver. Your giving commands heaven's attention if done properly and with the right motive.

By His grace, through our ministry my wife and I run a global charity initiative where we support missionaries and other charitable causes around the world. We help to build wells. We purchase shoes for children. We contribute to providing eye care for elderly people in Africa. This will not go unrewarded by God. That's what it means to extend the kingdom of God on the earth.

What are you doing apart from paying your tithes to advance and extend God's kingdom on earth? You must be committed to giving, not because you want to use your act of giving as a transactionary service to God, but because you love Him. Nothing provokes a harvest like giving out of love. People don't care how much you know until they know how much you care.

When you give to God, you can do so in many ways:

- You can give to God by supporting projects and initiatives in your local church.
- You can give to God by sowing into missionary works in different parts of the world.
- You can give to God by sponsoring charitable causes in different parts of the world.
- You can give to God by helping the less privileged in society.
- You can give to God by supporting your nation through the development of social amenities.

These are just a few of several giving opportunities available to us. When you give to God, you are positioned to be blessed by God in the following ways:

- God can send people to give to you in return.
- God can give you unique ideas that will help you to make more money.
- God can protect you from sickness and diseases, making you and your family healthy.
- God can protect you from natural calamity, accidents, and disasters.
- God can give you favour with men in places of honour and influence.
- Above all, God will certainly keep a record of your giving in heaven, where your eternal rewards are guaranteed.

SUMMARY OF CHAPTER FIVE

1. The Abrahamic covenant is an eternal covenant. Why then should we disregard the practices of Abraham? The end of the old covenant didn't end the Abrahamic covenant. Consequently, tithing is ordained by God and applies to all New Testament believers.
2. Tithes are symbols of covenants. Everyone who gives tithes to God is fulfilling his portion of the Abrahamic covenant.
3. The original intent of tithing is to have food, or provision, in the storehouse.
4. When you pay tithes to your church, or to wherever you consider your storehouse (where God has led you to be fed and nourished spiritually), you are actually paying it to God in obedience to His word.
5. God is the best selector of your place of worship. God appoints pastors for His sheep. If you can trust God with the responsibility of your place of worship (as in a church), He will lead you to the right place.
6. The place that qualifies as your storehouse, where your tithes must go, is where God has appointed you and led you into.

7. You must be certain and convinced with proofs that you are being fed with knowledge and understanding of God's word in your church. If you are experiencing the opposite, God might not have led you there.

8. When you pay your tithes, God promises to rebuke the devourer for your sakes. He promises not to allow the devourer to destroy the fruits of your ground. He promises not to allow the devourer to make you cast your fruit before the appropriate time. He promises to open for you the windows of heaven, and pour out a blessing.

9. When heaven is opened over your life, it is an indication of the free flow of communication with the Holy Spirit. Every exploit in the Kingdom of God is provoked by revelation.

10. You must be strongly committed to giving to the cause of charity and to the cause of advancing the spread of the gospel all across the globe.

CHAPTER SIX

THE QUEST FOR WEALTH AND THE
SPIRIT OF MAMMON

No man can serve two masters: for either he will hate the one, and love the other; or else he will hold to the one, and despise the other. Ye cannot serve God and mammon. (Matthew 6:24)

I am a firm believer in everything Jesus taught and demonstrated in the Scriptures. I am a firm believer in everything the apostles taught and demonstrated in the Scriptures. In fact, the entire Bible is my GPS.

Many years back, I heard Dr. Frederick K.C. Price say on TV, "Every word in the scripture is truly stated, but every word is not a statement of truth." He was making reference to the fact that despite the entire Bible being God's will for us, not every action and behaviour in the Bible was put there by God for us to copy. We should not commit suicide, though Judas did the same! I hope you get my drift.

For the love of money is the root of all evil: which while some coveted after, they have erred from the faith, and pierced themselves through with many sorrows. (1 Timothy 6:10)

One of the subtlest perils that can befall any Christian is being possessed by the spirit of mammon. There is a very thin line between the genuine kingdom prosperity that comes from God and the satanic wealth that comes from mammon. The desire to be rich and prosperous isn't devilish. There is nothing evil in the desire to prosper financially. It is the motive behind this desire that must be tested. This is why the Bible picks on the matter of the love of money, and it being the root of all evil.

The love aspect is a matter of the heart, where motives are developed and processed. Once your heart is corrupted towards money, your motives will be wrong for acquiring it. I have identified several motives behind many people's desires to be rich.

Note that I've mentioned in previous sections that I believe in total prosperity, in line with God's word. We must concentrate on God's total prosperity package, which includes spiritual, intellectual, and physical prosperity. Actual possession of finances falls within the category of physical prosperity. Every other material blessing, such as sound health, falls within the same category of physical prosperity.

Now, what are some of these common motives for desiring to be rich financially?

NINE WRONG MOTIVES FOR THE DESIRE FOR WEALTH

- To have access to the good things of life, such as cars, houses, lands, clothes, and expensive holiday packages. Although there is nothing sinful about having these, the ultimate purpose for wealth acquisition is not to lay up material things.
- To be named among the richest in your family, community, city, state, nation, or even the world.
- To exercise control and influence over family members in a way that your word becomes law.
- To exercise control and influence over friends and colleagues in a way that your word becomes law.
- To attract or impress the opposite sex.
- To send your children to the best schools at any time and at any cost.
- To become a history maker and ultimately make a name for yourself.
- To oppress and punish people at will, at any time.
- To service your ego by exhibiting your wealth at every opportunity in a way that creates fame for you.

Do you find your motive slotted in the list? If your answer is yes, you need to read this chapter very patiently. Almost all of these motives are wrong, with the exception of the first point. There is nothing really wrong with desiring money to access the good things of life. However, when it becomes the only driver for financial prosperity, it becomes a stronghold. In other words, a Christian doesn't live to constantly desire wealth to gather the good things of life. Having a "collection" mentality is not Christ-like.

WHAT IS MAMMON?

No man can serve two masters: for either he will hate the one, and love the other; or else he will hold to the one, and despise the other. Ye cannot serve God and mammon. (Matthew 6:24)

- The word mammon was taken by medieval writers as the name of the devil of covetousness. It comes from the Greek word *mammonas.*
- Scholars cite mammon as the name of a Syrian and Chaldean god, similar to the Greek god of wealth, Plutus.
- Mammon is used to describe all lusts and excesses: gluttony, greed, and dishonest worldly gain. Ultimately, mammon is an idol of materialism which many trust as a foundation for their world and philosophy.
- The worship of mammon can show up in many ways. It isn't always through a continual lust for more money, but through the envy of others' wealth.
- Mammon is a wicked spirit that grips and enslaves people through the medium of money.
- Mammon also describes a wicked spirit that operates through money. It causes people to bow down to money, worshiping it.
- Mammon makes people replace God with money by allowing it to rule every aspect of their lives.

Jesus makes it clear that serving God and mammon is mutually exclusive. This means, both cannot be done at the same time. The spirit of mammon is at the root of the nine motives of money described above.

Simply put, if your motive for money is among the list shown, you might have been captured by the spirit of mammon.

But can a Christian be captured by the spirit of mammon? Yes, of course. Not just the spirit of mammon, but by any other spirit, if such a Christian willfully steps outside of the cover of the Holy Spirit. Truly, a Christian cannot be possessed by another spirit for as long as he is still in Christ. However, we have seen many cases of believers willfully going into the camp of Satan for power, money, and favours of some sort. There have been cases of Christians who engaged willfully in acts of immorality and, after a long period of time, the Holy Spirit was grieved and another spirit began to work in the life of those Christians.

There is the wealth that comes from God. There is the wealth that comes from mammon. You need to see the motives God expects every Christian to have in their hearts for their quest for money. Check up this list to determine if this motive has ever been at the root of your prayer and fasting for financial prosperity.

Seven Godly Motives for the Desire for Wealth
- To invest in the discovery and fulfillment of your life's dream and purpose.
- To help the needy and less privileged in society through the provision of food, clothing, shelter, education, and healthcare services.
- To help your church meet their God-given kingdom expansion projects as the Lord helps.
- To invest in the development of viable charity projects that can help eradicate poverty.
- To give to the cause of revival, missions, and evangelism across the earth.
- To promote the success of other people's visions and dreams as the Lord leads you.

Now, I don't have a problem with anyone owning a hundred jets if those jets aren't just acquired to service the ego and pride of the owner. But they must truly contribute to any of the above godly motives for wealth acquisition. Kenneth E. Hagin used to say that there are many people who are poor, yet are consumed with the spirit of mammon. They are only seeking an opportunity to gain wealth, and then you will see their true colours. Maybe the reason God has not answered the prayers of many Christians in spite of their enormous giving is due to the motives of their hearts. Change your motives and God will change His mind. Many Christians have not yet matured to the point of being trusted with enormous wealth.

IF GOD WILL JUDGE UNPRODUCTIVITY WITH HELL, HOW WOULD HE JUDGE LUST?

I don't think any Christian or preacher who is consumed by the spirit of mammon can enter heaven. You see, many of us think that only adultery and stealing can send people to hell. Perish the thought. Just being unproductive is enough to send a man to hell. Remember the story of the talents told by Jesus? The master told his servants to throw the man with the one talent into outer darkness where there would be weeping and gnashing of teeth. That is hell. The man did not commit adultery. He was only unproductive. If God will judge unproductivity with hell, how would He judge lust? We must straighten up as God's people and change our attitude towards money and material possessions. You can have as much as you want, but you must not consume them of your own lust.

You are simply a steward with God. You must wisely invest and apply your resources to the advancement of God's kingdom on earth. Just like Pastor Sunday Adelaja mentioned in his revolutionary book *Kingdom Driven Life*, the kingdom of God is not a church. We are talking about something bigger than the body of Christ; we are referring to the economy of the kingdom, the culture of the kingdom, the members of the kingdom, and everything a kingdom is usually noted for. In other words, the wealth you desire from God must make an enormous impact on every sphere of influence God has given you in such a way that every aspect of God's kingdom is positively affected as much as God has given you grace. Your impact on earth must be commensurate with your size of wealth.

YOUR IMPACT ON
EARTH MUST BE
COMMENSURATE
WITH YOUR SIZE OF
WEALTH.

Are you labouring to store up wealth? Are you like some political office holder who sees political appointments as opportunities to steal and loot? Do you see money-making as your primary reason for living, or do you see it as a tool for fulfilling your assignment on earth? These are two different drives. What you are driving at is different from what is driving you. If you're being driven by an unholy passion for wealth, even at the expense of your name and credibility, then the spirit of mammon has taken a hold of you. Money should never be the main motivator for living. You must never get to a point where you shout the words, "I must make money at all costs." Your language as a Christian should be, "I must make money at God's cost."

The Bible makes it clear that we must not labour to be rich. In other words, don't be caught up in the web of struggle for the acquisition of wealth. Wealth doesn't come to God's children by labour. It comes by favour. Dr. Mike Murdock once said on TV, "Anywhere there is honour, there would be favour, and anywhere there is favour, there would be money." Simply put, finances flow in the direction of God's favour. You can't just sleep at home every day and pray for favour when you're not working. Only poverty will flow towards your direction if you live like that.

SUMMARY OF CHAPTER SIX

1. Kingdom wealth that comes from God is different from worldly wealth that comes from mammon.
2. Mammon is used to describe all lusts and excesses: gluttony, greed, and dishonest worldly gain. Ultimately, mammon is an idol of materialism, which many trust as a foundation for their world and philosophy.
3. Your impact on earth must be commensurate with your amount of wealth.
4. If God will judge unproductivity with hell, how would he judge

lust? Being possessed with the spirit of mammon can send a person to hell.

5. The wealth you desire from God must make an enormous impact on every sphere of influence God has given you in such a way that every aspect of God's kingdom is positively affected as much as God has given you grace.

6. Regardless of how much money you give to God, you don't qualify for financial empowerment from God if your motive is wrong.

7. The motive behind your quest for money determines if you are being controlled by the spirit of God or the spirit of mammon.

8. There is nothing evil in the desire to prosper financially. It is the motive behind this desire that must be tested.

CHAPTER SEVEN

Wealth of the Church and Societal
Transformation

Ye are the light of the world. A city that is set on an hill cannot be hid. (Matthew 5:14)

The Purpose of Wealth in the Church

What is the purpose of the enormous wealth of the church? Why do you think God has empowered His church with amazing wealth and resources? Of course, the answer is not farfetched: to be a light in this dark world. We now live at a critical time in history when some churches are richer than many nations. God has opened the windows of heaven on churches to the extent that churches now build and sustain universities, and operate charitable organizations whose budgets run into several millions (even billions) of dollars.

We live in a world where churches own TV stations, restaurants, shopping outlets, and commercial and residential real estate businesses. My job here is not to criticize the wealth of the church, but rather to direct our focus to the true purpose of this wealth and to the right source of generating and sustaining it. This is against the background that not all wealth in our churches comes from God, and not all wealth is used to glorify God and extend His kingdom. For those who have acquired wealth in ungodly ways, I strongly encourage you to repent and turn your eyes away from mammon to the only living God from whom real, authentic, lasting wealth comes.

I don't believe in the gospel that teaches believers to become and remain poor as a condition to make it to heaven. I strongly believe that wealth is a tool from God that can be used to fulfill our purpose on earth, while advancing the kingdom of God through the preaching of the gospel and providing for the millions of people in need. Let me make it plain: I don't care who has taught you that poverty is from God; you will be miserable in this world if you are poor.

WEALTH IS A TOOL FROM GOD THAT CAN BE USED TO FULFILL OUR PURPOSE ON EARTH,

Not everyone is controlled by money. There are still many people using their God-given wealth to help others, while living very simple and humble lives on earth. We must never get to the point of generalizing that financial prosperity leads to destruction and sends men to hell. We need money to extend God's kingdom. That is as simple as I can put it. We must not shy away from this fact.

My ministry's outreaches in Canada and in other parts of the world have been slowed down recently, owing to lack of sufficient funds. God has used our ministry to be a blessing to many people around the world. We have contributed to the provision of clean water to many children in sub-Saharan Africa. We have purchased shoes for many children in other parts of the world. We have contributed to sustaining our fellow brethren in underground churches in the Middle East. How would all of this have been done if we were poor and tattered? Would a man struggling to feed himself be able to help other struggling people?

It is the number one mark of selfishness to desire to remain poor or average. That means you have already placed a limit above your ability to help others. Only those of us in the church who are thinking about the number of houses we can live in or the number of shoes we need see wealth as unnecessary. But for believers out there who want a thousand shoes because they need two pairs and are ready to ship 998 to other people around the world? Supernatural wealth cannot elude them.

Pastor Sunday Adelaja was once accused of living in a mansion in the Ukraine with several rooms. During a TV appearance, the man of God replied his critics like this: "I and my family live in two rooms and give out several other rooms to missionaries and the needy in my society or anyone who has accommodation problems." He actually prepared ahead of time by building a house with scores of rooms. It takes a man with a large heart to live like that.

Another man of God, Bishop David Oyedepo, has been used amazingly by God to make an enormous impact on many lives, although he rarely talks about it, making people think he doesn't help others with his God-given wealth. More than ten children have been adopted by this man of God. They bare his surname. This is apart from tens of thousands of others who are employed in his organization or receive scholarships for their secondary and tertiary education. When he was on a trip outside Nigeria a couple of years ago, an unknown person approached him at the airport and asked assistance for his child who needed money for surgery at an Indian hospital. Oyedepo, right on the spot, issued a cheque for twenty-seven thousand euros. That was not reported by any media in Nigeria or in any other nation. Only his errors and weaknesses are reported.

That is the purpose of wealth. Regardless of the ills in the church of Christ, in terms of money and the prosperity gospel, there is still value in the financial practices of many wealthy ministries. The story isn't all negative.

I don't believe that the prosperity message is evil. I only disagree with those who preach it as if it's the only aspect of the gospel. The gospel is multifaceted and must be balanced at all times.

Let's look at some examples.

CHURCH OF ENGLAND

The latest available statistics indicate that

- 1 in 4 primary schools and 1 in 16 secondary schools in England are Church of England schools... Approximately 1 million pupils are educated in more than 4,700 Church of England schools.[9]
- Over 80,000 volunteers and around 2,700 Church Staff help provide support and activities for children, young people and families.[10]
- The Church of England has a long and successful history of involvement in education and schooling. As a statutory provider

---

[9] *The Church of England*, "Facts and Statistics." Date of access: May 5, 2016 (https://www.churchofengland.org/about-us/facts-stats.aspx).
[10] Ibid.

of schooling, the Church has built a very strong and respected position in England and Wales.

WORLD CHANGERS MINISTRIES, UNITED STATES

According to the ministry's website:

Care for Kids—where we address the physical, educational, emotional and spiritual needs of some of the most vulnerable children around the world. From South Africa to Thailand, we have been able to provide meals, shoes and clothing, medical attention and supplies, hygiene kits and personal education.

Hope in Disaster—which is dedicated to serving the needs of international- and domestic communities devastated by natural disasters. Alongside our on-the-ground partners, in both Nepal and Haiti, we have supported those affected by providing them with immediate basic needs such as shelter, clothes, toiletries and food.

Project Virtue—which supports Pastor Taffi's heart to restore the dreams and renewing the spirits of hurt, abandoned, and abused women around the world. From Canada to South Africa, we are committed to making a mark in the lives of these women – spiritually, emotionally and physically.

Love Thy Neighbour—where we are dedicated to doing grace-based, noble work for our neighbours around the world. We are empowering change in Kenya through Total Tribal Transformation, which includes building greenhouses to provide a sustainable source of food and clean water.[11]

TRIUMPHANT ENTRY MISSIONS INTERNATIONAL, SOUTH AFRICA

TEMI is a South-African-based Christian ministry at the forefront of changing the lives of the destitute in South Africa. Pictures don't lie. I worked with them for a short while, and here are some of the activities of this great organization at a glance.

[11] *Creflo Dollar Global Missions*, "Welcome to Creflo Dollar Global Mission." Date of access: May 5, 2016 (http://missions.creflodollarministries.org/CDGM/awelcomemessagefromcreflodollar).

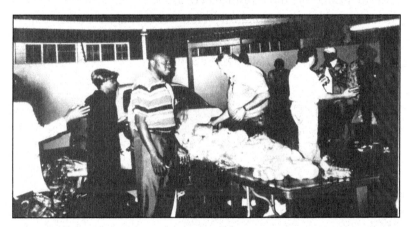

Those guys on the queue were picked from the streets, fed, clothed, and trained to become better citizens of South Africa. TEMI spends a lot of money on this project. Who would these great people of South Africa have turned to if TEMI had been too poor to extend a hand of fellowship to them? This is what is called practical Christian ministry. It's exactly what Jesus would do if He were still physically on earth.

WATER FOR LIFE MINISTRIES, UNITED STATES

The above picture shows the activity of Water for Life Ministries, which my own ministry has been part of for a couple of years. Prior to their involvement, these great children drank dirty water from the river. Now they can smile at the gushing of clean water because of the financial investment of a Christian ministry. How would Jesus have behaved if He were still present on the earth? This is what financial empowerment does to those who have God's wisdom for using it.

CANADA FOOD BANK, CANADA

The above pictures show Pastor Sunday Adebamiro and his wife, missionaries to the nations of the world. They now live in Canada and have been supplying free bread to hungry people as a means of sharing the gospel. Their ministry has been used tremendously to bless thousands of homes. They have supplied free bread to people in Libya, Cuba, the Bahamas, and in many other nations.

TELAVISION, NIGERIA

Telavision is run by a Nigerian-based Christian organization. They go into rural communities and provide free eye treatments to people with eye problems. They have taken care of so many people who would have gone blind otherwise. This project costs them a lot of money, and they have invested massively in extending the project to other African nations.

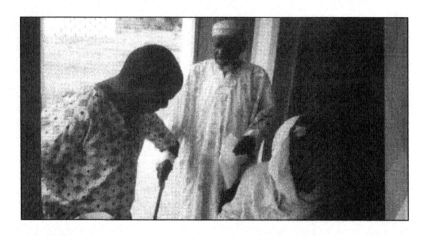

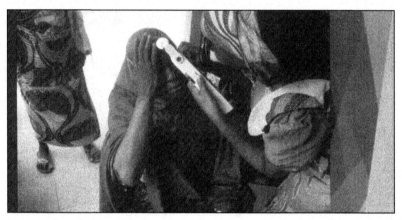

Bridge of Hope, United States

- In Guatemala, 275,000 meals and $250,000 in medical supplies have been delivered to one of the poorest nations on the earth.

- In El Salvador, an earthquake left one million people homeless. Bridge of Hope provided immediate shelter for twenty thousand of them.
- In Haiti, the poorest country in the western hemisphere, Bridge of Hope delivered three hundred thousand pounds of food and medical supplies.

There is no better way to show the love of Christ in a dark world than to use our God-given wealth to change the lives of others.

EMBASSY OF THE BLESSED KINGDOM OF GOD, UKRAINE

Pastor Sunday Adelaja serves as a case study of his own. What God has used his church to do in Ukraine is worth celebrating, but this book will not be able to do justice to the activities of this great church, which has practically revolutionized an entire nation.

As of 2004, my good friend Pastor Derek Schneider compiled some of the activates of this great church in his amazing book, *Beyond the Four Walls*.

Among several other projects of the church, the following had been executed by the end of 2014:

- Over seventy million people were led to Christ between 1994 and 2014.

- Over a thousand churches were planted in over fifty countries.
- Over seven hundred non-government organizations (NGOs) and 235 rehabilitation centres have been opened.
- 36,456 people have been ministered to at the rehabilitation centres.
- 3,846,189 people have been ministered to at social churches.
- Three thousand leaders have ministered at the church in Kiev.
- 273 education centres have been established around the world.
- Between one and two thousand people are fed daily in the church's soup kitchen.
- Over ten thousand people have been set free from drug and alcohol addiction, and over forty-three thousand parents of drug addicts have passed through the church's rehabilitation programs.
- The lives of 68,382 homeless, disabled, orphan, or crisis-ridden children have been transformed.
- Over 47,245 elderly people have been cared for.
- Over three thousand organizations have been established by church members across the cities of the Ukraine.
- The radio and television ministry reaches over one hundred million people weekly throughout Europe, Russia, and Africa.
- Five hundred homeless or abandoned children have been restored to their families.
- Political leaders attend the church regularly.
- Thousands of mafia members have come to Christ.
- The church's hotline has counselled over seventy thousand people, of which 1,500 are now church members.
- Many schools for ministry have been established.
- Hundreds of thousands of Christians have impacted all spheres of life and society.
- The ministry received 154 awards in 2014 alone from presidents, ministries, and local governments.[12]

[12] Derek Schneider, *Beyond the Four Walls: From Revival to Societal Transformation* (Toronto, ON: Conclusio, 2014), 48–50.

Redeemed Christian Church of God (City of David Parish, Lagos, Nigeria)

Among several thousands parishes of the RCCG church is the City of David, popularly called COD, and based in Lagos. For many years, this church has contributed immensely to the advancement of God's kingdom in Nigerian society. Here are some of the ways:

- Construction of the Healing Striped Hospital, Dialysis, and Diagnostic Centre, offering thirty free dialysis sessions on a monthly basis to the tune of more than $1.5 million since its inception in 2013.
- The Arise Women Mobile Medical Clinic, established for the sum of more than $250,000, leading to the provision of free medical treatments for close to eight thousand people since its inception.
- The introduction of a poverty alleviation program that has fed up to sixty thousand people since its inception and has cost the church more than two million dollars.
- The establishment of a rehabilitation centre for commercial sex workers and substance abusers.
- The installation of forty-eight solar street lights across different parts of the city.

- The church started the God's Children Got Talent program, for children between the ages of three and twenty.
- The provision of equipment to more than 125 schools in Nigeria, leading to the investment of more than three hundred thousand dollars on educational projects and scholarship programs.
- The church donated boreholes, medicines, generators, and ambulances to organisations throughout Nigeria.

At the moment, the City of David parish is engaged in the construction of a major facility that will further contribute to the expansion of their numerous charity projects. The proposed services associated with this facility are as follows:

- The facility will include twelve passenger lifts, a concert hall for five thousand people, a mechanical room for each tower, two cinema halls, a medical centre, a recreation theme park, a shopping centre, and a 100-seat restaurant.
- An adjoining multi-storey car park for approximately 670 cars.
- A state-of-the-art audio-visual facility suitable for live broadcasts.
- Tenant-dedicated external garden terraces protected by a lattice frame structure.
- The building's orientation maximizes natural light and ventilation and minimizes solar exposure, reducing the energy requirements for cooling, heating, and air quality.

Isn't this amazing? This is a clear picture of what it means to impact society with the wealth of the church. The COD is just one parish, with thousands of other parishes of the RCCG ministry making enormous investments towards societal transformation, some of which include the Jesus House Church located in Toronto, Canada.

IS THE CHURCH USING ITS WEALTH TO DO ENOUGH IN THE WORLD?

A lot of people have been speaking out recently about the fact that there's a mismatch between the volume of wealth at the disposal of the church and the contribution of the church to society. I share the same sentiment, partially. Using education as a major case study, I agree that the church of Christ should invest massively in providing affordable education to as many people as can afford it. However, what is affordable to one party might not be for another. Taking Africa as an example, the extent of poverty in many nations often makes it difficult to accurately estimate the relationship between value and cost of education. For example, in many places of Nigeria, Ethiopia, Ghana, Cameroon, Tanzania, South Africa, the Congo, and other societies in west, south, and east Africa, the level of poverty is huge. Many churches have started running private universities, charging fees that have been the subject of contention in many circles. The question is this: should a church be profit-oriented in its university project? For that matter, should a church make profit in any of its endeavours? I think it depends on the context. Jesus never spoke against having a profit mentality. He didn't judge it at all. However, when a church misplaces its focus on evangelism, care for society, love for people, and free will contributions to the emancipation of society, becoming entangled with its passion for business, we need to raise an eyebrow.

In very poor African nations, churches need to be careful to balance their appetite for profit maximization and society emancipation and transformation. Can an average citizen of your society afford the cost of your services, be it education, health, or whatever? If they would need to bleed to afford the cost, making you a profit in the process, there's a problem. It is ungodly to bleed people to pay for a service. Jesus would never be involved in such a business venture. A church of Christ should be like Christ and use its resources to make an impact on society in a manner that doesn't put pressure on people.

> IT IS UNGODLY TO BLEED PEOPLE TO PAY FOR A SERVICE. JESUS WOULD NEVER BE INVOLVED IN SUCH A BUSINESS VENTURE.

Now, I don't mean that people shouldn't pay for services rendered by the church, but we must be very careful not to inflict more pain on poor people in our quest to make profit. Hear what the Holy Spirit has to say:

Pure religion and undefiled before God and the Father is this, To visit the fatherless and widows in their affliction, and to keep himself unspotted from the world. (James 1:27)

In Nigeria, a lot of churches own universities and other service outlets. Many people complain that they're bleeding to send their children to schools owned by churches in Nigeria. If the proportion of such people outweighs the proportion of people paying for the service comfortably, then we need to wake up. Jesus would not run a university or render any service that would make people cry and wail to pay for it. In John 6:1, Jesus was so compassionate to the people that He told the apostles to find them something to eat. The apostles declined on the grounds that they didn't have enough and Jesus should send them away. Jesus didn't approve of their recommendation. A pastor in another part of the world might have sent them away hungry. This story is very instructive. Jesus would never put people under pain or affliction of any kind, regardless of what He would lose to do so.

What am I saying here? Services that are rendered by the church must be priced in a way that doesn't put more affliction and pressure on people. That is what will make our light shine. How easy would it be to preach the gospel to the Islamic community in Ethiopia if a church decided to give scholarships to students from Islamic backgrounds in their first year? Our desires and appetite for profit must never outweigh our desire to draw people into the kingdom through our behaviour and attitudes.

OUR DESIRES AND APPETITE FOR PROFIT MUST NEVER OUTWEIGH OUR DESIRE TO DRAW PEOPLE INTO THE KINGDOM THROUGH OUR BEHAVIOUR AND ATTITUDES.

Many churches charge exorbitant fees for a university education, causing the church of Christ to be criticized. Do not take what I'm saying out of context. A university education should be paid for by those who can afford it. The quality must be justified by the fees, no doubt about it. The cost to run a university must be compensated for by revenue. Very logical and sound. But not at the expense of poor people. If you're running a service in a relatively rich society, you are at liberty to charge fees that are commensurate with the standard of living in that society.

If thou lend money to any of my people that is poor by thee, thou shalt not be to him as an usurer, neither shalt thou lay upon him usury. (Exodus 22:25)

Take thou no usury of him, or increase: but fear thy God; that thy brother may live with thee. (Leviticus 25:36)

He that by usury and unjust gain increaseth his substance, he shall gather it for him that will pity the poor. (Proverbs 28:8)

Did you see anything in the above scriptures? For churches who offer services in societies where people are above average and can pay, there is nothing wrong in making a profit and becoming rich from the proceeds. However, the Lord is not pleased when we profit from poor people. It is offensive to God. So many churches are making profits this way. They're just wasting their time. The leaders are making a date with the judgement of God. It's only a matter of time.

Read with me this dialogue:

PASTOR: The Lord has given me a vision to start a university that will benefit all of us as a church. We must all contribute money to build this university. It is our heritage for life.

CHURCH MEMBER: I borrowed money from a bank to contribute my quota to the building of this university, but now my son cannot afford the tuition fees. I thought our pastor said we would all benefit from it.

That is the sad state of some churches. The purpose of wealth in the church is to make life more comfortable to hurting and poor people, to extend God's kingdom on earth by investing in causes that will improve the wellbeing of the church, society, and the kingdom of God at large. For churches that run hospitals, universities, and other social services, our desire for wealth and riches must never consume us beyond the need to be a light in a dark world. Wealth is a tool in the hand of a church to draw millions of people to the kingdom of God regardless of what it will cost to achieve that.

SUMMARY OF CHAPTER SEVEN

1. The purpose of wealth in the church is to make life more comfortable to hurting and poor people, to extend God's kingdom on earth by investing in causes that will improve the wellbeing of the church, society, and the kingdom of God at large.

2. I don't believe that the prosperity message is evil. I only disagree with those who preach it as if it's the only aspect of the gospel. The gospel is multifaceted and must be balanced at all times.

3. Jesus never spoke against having a profit mentality. He didn't judge it at all. However, when a church misplaces its focus on evangelism, care for society, love for people, and free will contributions to the emancipation of society, becoming entangled with its passion for business, we need to raise an eyebrow.

4. The services you render as a church, or as a Christian individual, shouldn't make people bleed to pay for it.

5. A church of Christ should be like Christ and use its resources to make an impact on society in a manner that doesn't put pressure on people.

6. Our desires and appetites for profit and wealth must never outweigh our desire to draw people into the kingdom through our behaviour and attitudes.

CHAPTER EIGHT

WE ARE THE JESUS OF
OUR GENERATION

In my Father's house are many mansions: if it were not so, I would have told you. I go to prepare a place for you. And if I go and prepare a place for you, I will come again, and receive you unto myself; that where I am, there ye may be also. (John 14:2–3, emphasis added)

THE PERIL OF PROMOTING SATAN ABOVE JESUS IN OUR CHURCHES

Of all the evils confronting the body of Christ globally, the lack of knowledge of who believers are seems to top the list. Having lived in two different generations of Christians, I have, by the grace of God, been able to draw clear lines of distinction between who Christians perceived themselves to be more than thirty years ago and who they perceive themselves to be now.

The Lord gave me an early start, and I was privileged to know Christ more than thirty years ago. Those days were widely tagged as the SU (Scripture Union) days in Nigeria. Today, messages that promote Satan and his power dominate our altars. Many pastors dedicate the vast majority of their time talking about Satan and how powerful he is, neglecting the focus on a balanced gospel that cuts Satan down to size, while showing God's people their actual status and position in Christ.

The reasons for that are quite clear. Churches that promote deliverance and supernatural signs and wonders seem to attract a larger crowd than those that focus on other messages. Many Christians forget that sign and wonders can be adulterated by Satan. The presence of a crowd at church, or the presence of signs and wonders, doesn't validate that church.

It may sound strange, but there are cases of churches in Africa—and throughout the world—where unusual spiritual occurrences happen. Ultimately, these negative practices influence the lives of believers.

Of course, I believe in signs and wonders, and God has used our ministry in this area. To Him alone be the glory. But we don't put the cart before the horse. We major on feeding people with the word, while allowing the word to do what only He can do. Jesus Himself is the word of God personified.

Signs and wonders don't produce lasting fruits in people. Only the word that is received has the potential to set men free. Many churches have the problem that when they don't feed the people with God's word through variety of training and teaching programs, they raise members that depend on pastors—members who can't confront Satan and cut him down to size. They raise members who fall cheaply into sin and bring shame and disgrace to the name of the Lord. They raise carnal members who are only looking for prophecies and solutions to their problems.

Numerous church founders and pastors dominate their members by not letting them know who they are in Christ. The same mindset influences the way they spend and make money.

YOU WERE SAVED TO EXTEND GOD'S KINGDOM ON EARTH, NOT JUST GO TO HEAVEN

I was stunned for days when the Holy Spirit opened my eyes to an amazing revelation. For many years, we have interpreted John 14:2–3 to refer to our eventual exit out of this world to mansions built by the Lord Jesus in heaven. I believe firmly in that doctrine. It is perfectly scriptural that there is a mansion waiting for us in heaven. However, the Holy Spirit turned those scriptures around and blew them up in my spirit. *"In my Father's house are many mansions"* (John 14:2). The word "mansion" stands for rooms or opportunities or capacities, while the word "house" stands for the kingdom of God. So what that scripture is saying is this: "In my Father's kingdom are many opportunities."

Isn't that amazing? Opportunities to become what? Opportunities to discover your purpose and fulfill it. Opportunities to become great and excellent. Jesus didn't save us to escape out of this world, otherwise we would have died the same day we were born again. Why is God keeping us alive even after we gave our lives to Jesus? To discover His purpose for our lives and extend His kingdom on earth.

The church of Christ is not the kingdom of God. We often mix up these two words. Understanding this difference will help you to see a bigger picture of our role as Christians in influencing every aspect of our society with the principles of God kingdom.

You Are at the Same Level with Jesus

But how can a set of people who don't even know their right and position in God influence this world? It takes changed men to change societies. You can't give what you don't have. This is the main purpose of my book.

I go to prepare a place for you. And if I go and prepare a place for you, I will come again, and receive you unto myself. (John 14:2–3)

"I go to prepare a place for you" is a prophecy Jesus fulfilled in death. He went to the cross to prepare a room for you and me in the kingdom. What Jesus did on the cross is far greater and deeper than what many of us presently understand. He didn't just save you to go to heaven; He saved you to save your world. He saved you to permeate and influence your society and your spheres of influence with kingdom values.

Secondly, the above scripture says something further: "I will come again." Wow. That is deeper than the rapture. Jesus was saying to us that He would resurrect again. "I will come again" refers to His resurrection from the grave. In other words, the first three statements should be read like this: "In my Father's kingdom are many opportunities. I am going to die on the cross and rise again on the third day to open you up to those opportunities."

Now, wait a minute. The Holy Spirit blew me up completely by the last phrase of June 14:3—*"that where I am, there ye may be also."* Do you see something in that scripture? It says something deeper than merely dying and going to heaven to be where Jesus is. Jesus is saying something fundamentally critical to our dominion on earth. "That where I am, there ye may be also." In other words, the original intention of God is to put us at the same level with Jesus!

Jerry Savelle shared an amazing story about the above principle on a TV teaching for Daystar Television. He opened the frontiers of wisdom on who we are in Christ, by quoting the following verse:

> *I in them, and thou in me, that they may be made perfect in one; and that the world may know that thou hast sent me,* and hast loved them, as thou hast loved me. (John 17:23, emphasis added)

So God loves us the same way He loves Jesus. Savelle blew everyone into shreds with this amazing revelation. Some religious people will find that statement disturbing, but I'll repeat it again: you were saved to be elevated on the same level as Jesus. You and Jesus are at the same level. I'm not saying that we have become saviours of the world, but by redemption we have been made to be the Jesuses of this world. The main Jesus is in heaven, but the other Jesuses are now on earth. These are those who have accepted His finished work on the cross by grace and have given their lives to him.

Now, if you and I are the Jesuses of this world, we wouldn't have any issue with how to acquire or spend money. Very simple, Jesus would feed the multitude even with scarce resources. You and I should do the same. Jesus would never encourage oppression of the poor or downtrodden. Neither would He endorse merchandising the people of God in any church.

WHERE IS JESUS AT THIS PRESENT MOMENT?

> *And what is the exceeding greatness of his power to us-ward who believe, according to the working of his mighty power, which he*

wrought in Christ, when he raised him from the dead, and set him at his own right hand in the heavenly places, far above all principality, and power, and might, and dominion, and every name that is named, not only in this world, but also in that which is to come: and hath put all things under his feet, and gave him to be the head over all things to the church... (Ephesians 1:19–22)

Do you see where Jesus is seated? Can you see the position of our Lord Jesus? He is far above all witches or powers or principalities of any kind. Even when He was in a boat on the brink of capsizing, He was in charge. He was sleeping. That's where Jesus wants us to be. He said, "Where I am, there you might be also." Stop running from pillar to post looking for prayer contractors to pray for you against Satan. You are not at his level.

And hath raised us up together, and made us sit together in heavenly places in Christ Jesus... (Ephesians 2:6)

You were saved and repositioned by God to operate at the same level with Jesus. Come on, wake up and change your perception about yourself. Satan is afflicting you because you haven't discovered your true position, *"[for] my people are destroyed for lack of knowledge"* (Hosea 4:6).

I announce to you, friends, that you are not beaten and battered. Your position is right beside Jesus, and you are far from witches and wizards and generational curses and generational crises. That was part of the package delivered by Jesus on the cross. But if you don't know, Satan will rob you and make mockery of your right. Stand up and call his bluff and you will see radical changes in your life. Once Satan knows that you have discovered your authority and position in Christ, he will move on. He can't stand revelation.

> YOU WERE SAVED AND REPOSITIONED BY GOD TO OPERATE AT THE SAME LEVEL WITH JESUS.

Jesus's original intention for you is this: "Where I am, there you may be also." If that is the case, we should come back and review the lifestyle of Jesus. Would He set a university with a tuition fee of a million dollars? It wouldn't even be a question. Everything about Jesus would epitomize love, care, and compassion.

The church of Christ around the world must rise up and take its true position in society, routing the devil out of our minds, setting the pace, and blazing the trail in advancing and extending God's kingdom in the way we live our lives and in the way we make and spend money.

SUMMARY OF CHAPTER EIGHT

1. Of all the evils confronting the body of Christ globally, the lack of knowledge of who we are as believers seems to top the list.
2. Many Christians forget that signs and wonders can be adulterated by Satan. The presence of a crowd at church, or the presence of signs and wonders, does not validate that church.
3. He saved you to save your world. He saved you to permeate and influence your society and spheres of influence with kingdom values.
4. The original intention of God is to put us at the same level as Jesus!
5. God loves you exactly the same way He loves Jesus.

CHAPTER NINE

SOURCES OF FINANCES FOR MINISTRIES
AND CHURCHES

Of all the burdens in the hearts of those God has called to full or part-time fivefold ministry offices, it seems that the matter of finance is the most critical. Not that other issues related to obeying the voice of God and seeking Him aren't important, but the financial pressure that confronts many in ministry has pushed ministers into temptation. We will deal with the temptations and problems that presently confront ministers of the gospel in subsequent sections. In this twenty-first century, it seems like the manner in which ministries and the preaching of the gospel must be done differs remarkably from how it was done many decades ago.

Financial provisions continue to be a major variable of concern and interest to all and sundry. This is against the background that almost every assignment given to a minister of the gospel consumes resources at different phases and stages. Resources can be in the form of people, money, material, intellectual capabilities, technology, and infrastructure, among others.

At this present moment in the history of the church, the most common sources of finances are:

• Tithes and offerings.
• Special seeds and pledges.
• Prophet offerings and gifts to ministers.
• Special financial commitments from partners.

The vast majority of churches and ministries depend on the above. Other churches and ministries have expanded this traditional list to include:

- Sales of Christian literature, music albums, CDs, and other electronic versions of messages.
- Income from training and Bible colleges.
- The establishment of universities, hospitals, and other service-driven initiatives.

There is nothing wrong with any of these sources. But the motive and spirit behind them matters to God, and no church or pastor must deviate from having God at the centre of every initiative. Only if God isn't glorified in any of these sources can issues be raised against them. Many ministers of the gospel have in recent times veered off the radar by going to Satan to collect supernatural powers to raise finances. They still use the above methods to launder their satanic activities. But at the root of their financial success is the power of Satan.

Again, note that these strange acts may be hard to accept for many Christians in the western world. But they are real, and their ultimate influence on churches and believers is negative.

SATANIC INFLUENCES IN CHURCH/MINISTRY FINANCES

In my few years of being a Christian, I have heard a lot of cases of satanic financial interventions for those who have consulted the devil. Shocking as it might be, that is the plain truth. So many people are parading themselves as pastors and bishops, but their sources of finances are nothing short of satanic.

Don't be deceived by the supernatural signs and wonders demonstrated by some ministries. Only the fruits of the spirit are sufficient for proving the authenticity of a ministry. Proofs via miracles and money are not reliable sources. Many pastors have made covenant with Satan for continuous financial supply. Such cases have been witnessed in different parts of the world. In almost all the cases, money and miracles go together. They are two sides of the same coin, and for those who patronize Satan, he gives both.

I once heard a story of a young minister whose church was located close to a senior minister and who was worried about the slow growth of his church despite years of labour. He went to the see the senior minister for counselling and the senior minister invited him to a so-called program where he could be taught on how to grow a big church. The trip landed this minister next to a massive ocean, and to the surprise of the young minister a mermaid came out of the waters and forced the young minister to have sexual intercourse with her. The young minister became very rich and extremely anointed after this ritual. A few years later, he was dead. The senior minister is still alive today.

Unbelievable? This is the tip of the iceberg. Never get to a point as a Christian or a minister where you are deceived to go to Satan for money—or for anything. That is the beginning of sorrow and destruction.

Their sorrows shall be multiplied that hasten after another god: their drink offerings of blood will I not offer, nor take up their names into my lips. (Psalms 16:4)

A minister of God I'm close to in Canada started a TV station and was approached by a Satanist to join their society if he desired wealth. He shared this with us at a meeting and spoke about the pressure he was put under by this group. He was told that they controlled the wealth of the nation of Canada and would give him anything he needed to become very rich. Of course he declined to join.

Strange though this may sound, it actually happened to an African man living in Canada.

I have personally had a revelation of a woman who came to me asking me to stretch out my hand for the power to become wealthy. I declined and prayed about this vigorously. Many pastors have been trapped by Satan just because of their unholy appetite for money and finances. They have allowed the love of money to entrap them, the end is always destruction and sorrow.

For the love of money is the root of all evil: which while some coveted after, they have erred from the faith, and pierced themselves through with many sorrows. (1 Timothy 6:10)

Why should you end your journey in sorrow? Whatever Satan does will always have an original copy with God. God never sends any man to the battlefield without thoroughly equipping him. You don't have to go to Satan for help in getting resources to fulfill your ministry.

God owns the original power for wealth. Grace is sufficient for your ministry. Your level of faithfulness with the grace given to you will determine the level of resources heaven will release into your life and ministry. God is faithful. He never sends anyone on any assignment He hasn't made absolute provision for. All He does is release these resources in phases and in levels.

And God is able to make all grace abound toward you; that ye, always having all sufficiency in all things, may abound to every good work... (2 Corinthians 9:8)

HOW DOES GOD SUPERNATURALLY RELEASE FINANCES TO A MINISTRY?

- God tests faithfulness and releases finances to ministries relative to their level of faithfulness
- God tests the heart and would always release finances whose sizes are commensurate to the level of spiritual maturity of a minister
- God uses men as channels of financial blessings to ministries
- God uses the anointing as channels of financial blessings to ministries
- God gives creative ministry ideas to men and women as sources of financial blessings to ministries

One of the most outstanding pictures of the pattern and order of God in releasing financial resources to ministers was revealed to me by the Holy Spirit. Join me in reading from John 21:

*And he said unto them, Cast the net on the right side of the ship,
and ye shall find. They cast therefore, and now they were not able
to draw it for the multitude of fishes. Therefore that disciple whom
Jesus loved saith unto Peter, It is the Lord. Now when Simon Peter
heard that it was the Lord, he girt his fisher's coat unto him, (for
he was naked,) and did cast himself into the sea. And the other
disciples came in a little ship; (for they were not far from land, but
as it were two hundred cubits,) dragging the net with fishes. As soon
then as they were come to land, they saw a fire of coals there, and
fish laid thereon, and bread.* (John 21:6–9)

This story offers immense insight into what God intentionally does
with His children prior to releasing resources to their ministries. After
the apostles saw Jesus in His true personality, something phenomenal
happened. Look at the last verse: *"As soon then as they were come to land,
they saw a fire of coals there, and fish laid thereon, and bread."* In Luke
5, the same experience plays out in another form. After Peter and the
apostles brought their boat to land, they forsook all and followed Christ.
But in this scenario, they saw something! The first thing they saw was
fire.

FIRE ENCOUNTERS

God will prosper no one financially, in ministry or in business, who
lacks the fire of God in his life. Fire stands for the anointing. Fire stands
for the power of God. Fire stands for the unction of the Holy Spirit.

I discovered that the Lord used fire encounters for many people
called into ministry. Moses was called through an encounter with fire.
Elijah was validated as a prophet by an encounter with fire. Isaiah had
an encounter with fire. The apostles weren't sent out until they had a fire
baptism in Acts 2.

As a minister of God, you should thirst for the power of God with
madness. Power exists at different levels, but I'm referring to the main
rod of your ministry. If you are a teacher of the word, you must carry a
supernatural power of teaching that will make you an enormous blessing
to the people of God. If you are a prophet, you must be so anointed so

you can see far and wide into the hearts of men as God gives you the privilege. Even if you're called to be a musician, you must be crazy for supernatural empowerment to sing and bring down the glory of God.

Fire has influence. No one ignores fire. Dare to be fired up and watch how the world gathers to watch and celebrate you. Notice that in John 21, the fish was laid on the fire. Fish are a symbol for men. Remember, Jesus told Peter in Luke 5 that He would make him a fisher of men.

FISH

I have never met or seen any man who carried the fire of God and lacked followers. Fire is a natural attractor of men. Jesus carried so much fire that he had to borrow boats to preach from the sea. The crowd was just too much.

You can't lack men in your life and ministry when you're on fire. But ministry isn't just limited to the preaching of the gospel. An athlete can carry the supernatural power of God and excel as a world-class athlete. Anybody with a ministry assignment who catches fire from God cannot lack men. You will be sought after. Now, remember John 21: after the fish was laid on the fire, bread showed up. Bread is a symbol of provision.

BREAD

Angels don't give money. Men do. It is eternally impossible for you to carry the fire of God, attract the right men into your life, and lack provision. The order has been laid down by God. When you're burning and shining, the fish run towards you. When the fish run towards you, bread follows.

Kenneth Hagin once shared a story of how he suffered for many years as a pastor until he discovered his right calling and was specially anointed by Jesus Himself. An eruption occurred in his ministry. Poverty died a natural death as the great man of God began to impact the lives of millions all over America and different parts of the world.

Mention any who's who in the history of the American church and see how the fire of God in their lives attracted fish. Notice that the fish Peter caught were 153 in number, and they were big fish. Stop running after money in ministry. If you put bread ahead of fish and fire, you'll be trapped by Satan and do anything to get money. If you put fish before fire, you'll be running after men and lose your integrity. The right order for sustainable and covenant-based divine financial empowerment is this:

What should be your ultimate source of financial blessing as a minister? Who should you seek for finances to complete the assignment given to you? God! Seek Him passionately and let Him empower you with His anointing and you can never be poor. My spiritual father, Bishop Francis Wale Oke, used to say, "The anointing may meet you poor, but it cannot leave you poor."

I'm not promoting the pursuit of money here. We need to direct our hearts to pursue God and His assignment and get empowered.

Remember, I said earlier that Satan never separates power from finances. They seem to go together. Even in the secular world, once people attain a certain position of power in government, resources and benefits begin to gravitate towards them. I implore you, friends, to take your eyes off men. Do not pursue money. Pursue God and get yourself at the cutting edge of His impact and watch how He embarrasses you with finances.

The evangelist Reinhard Bonnke once shared a story of how he lost his 35,000-seater tent to a terrible storm in Africa. He then went to a ministers conference organized by Kenneth Copeland. Right in the middle of their lunch, Copeland asked him a question. "I heard the news of the disaster that blew off your tent. How much would a new tent cost?" Reluctantly, Pastor Bonnke said, "Eight hundred thousand dollars." Brother Copeland said, "I'm giving you the money." But how did pastor Bonnke get to that level? He connected with the fire of God so that the miraculous became a norm at his meetings. That naturally drew men like Kenneth Copeland, and Kenneth Copeland was used by God to draw money into Pastor Bonnke's ministry.

Fire exist in levels. The fire of yesterday might not be enough for the exploits of today. You might need to relight the fire.

Kenneth E. Hagin was once asked about when he would retire. He told his audience, "I am not retiring. I am refiring." He did refire before he passed on. More than twelve years after being called to glory, his fire is still burning in the hearts of men around the world.

If your life isn't attracting the right type of men, check the intensity of your fire. Your fire might be going down. You might need to pay the price for a greater intensity of fire. In the seventeenth century, the great man of God John Wesley once said, "God sets me on fire in private; men watch me burn in the open."

Evangelist Leonard Ravenhill writes in his book *Why Revival Tarries* that secret prayer always results in short and powerful public prayer.[13] Your will naturally reproduce in public the kind of person you are in private. As fire comes in all sizes, so do fish. Everything in this world comes in different sizes.

Incidentally, God rarely releases everything you want at the same time. He is looking for men and women who would grow in the intensity of their fire. The higher the intensity, the greater the fish—and the bigger the bread. Stop complaining about the fish you are receiving. The problem is not with the fish, but with your fire.

Consider people in sports, music, the arts, and engineering. As soon as a person demonstrates a unique level of performance, club owners and music companies and promoters start looking for him. No footballer stays at the same level of skill. We watch the game of football, see how superstars like Cristiano Ronaldo have fared recently, and compare their performance to when they were teenagers. They grow in skills and talents, and as their talents and skills grow, they attract larger remuneration.

I want to conclude this section by encouraging you to thirst after the fire of God in your life, either as a minister of the gospel or a minister in the secular world. God never sends anyone on assignment and abandons them. He is too faithful to disappoint.

Stop pursuing the wrong thing. Money and men aren't the first priorities. Fire is the first priority. Let us pursue the fire. We will attract the fish, and the fish will bring the money.

---

[13] Leonard Ravenhill, *Why Revival Tarries* (Ada, MI: Bethany House, 2004).

Summary of Chapter Nine

1. It is possible for Satan to influence a minister of the gospel if care is not taken. There are ministers whose financial blessings actually come from Satan because they went to him.

2. Your level of faithfulness with the grace given to you will determine the level of resources that heaven will release into your life and ministry.

3. The Lord used fire encounters for many people called into ministry in Scripture. Fire stands for the anointing. Fire stands for the power of God. Fire stands for the unction of the Holy Spirit.

4. Fish stand for men. You can't lack men in your life and ministry when you're on fire for God.

5. When you're burning and shining, fish run towards you. When fish run towards you, bread follows the fish.

6. If you put bread ahead of fish and fire, you will be trapped by Satan and do anything to get money. If you put fish before fire, you will be running after men and lose your integrity. The right order for sustainable and covenant-based divine financial empowerment is fire, fish, and bread.

CHAPTER TEN

PERILS OF MAMMON IN THE
BODY OF CHRIST

A great man of God once visited a church in an African city and caused a stir. It was a holy stir. Almost everyone was on their knees weeping after this man of God finished preaching. He hit them below the belt with his message of repentance and consecration.

After the service, a very wealthy-looking gentleman approached the preacher and requested an appointment with him. The man of God agreed to see the man after the service. The wealthy man made a further special request to host him at his house where they could further discuss without any distractions. Reluctantly, the man of God agreed for a date.

When the day arrived, the man of God visited the wealthy man at his palatial home. Everything about the house smelled of wealth, opulence, and grandeur. The man of God was taken by this wealthy man into his private bedroom, and upon getting there the wealthy man told the man of God that he had a confession to make, and he just had to make it behind closed doors. The curiosity of the man of God was further awakened, and to his utmost surprise the wealthy man opened a secured door and revealed the dead body of his wife; it had been satanically preserved for money rituals.

The man of God was stunned. He asked the wealthy man if his pastor in the church was aware of this. The wealthy man answered yes. In fact, he mentioned that he had supported most projects in the church from proceeds from his demonic wealth. The man of God was stunned and stormed out of the house, only to be accosted by the wealthy man with some heavy cash.

The man of God turned it down and the wealthy man pulled out a gun to kill the man of God, having seen his secret. The man of God resisted the spirit and the wealthy man broke down in tears to repent. The man of God told him to go and make a public confession, and he also threatened never to preach on the altar of their church again.

Shocking? It is real and it happened in Africa, further suggesting the need for the true gospel of the kingdom to be preached across these regions on an ongoing basis.

That's exactly the feeling I had on hearing this story. This is the outcome of the operation of the spirit of mammon in the church, that a pastor would know that his member was a member of the occult, and had been made rich by the occult, and would still harbour him in the church and collect money from him. That is the extent to which the spirit of mammon can prevail over anyone who turns his back on God's prosperity. When the spirit of mammon grips a church, the results are terrible. Pastors will go to any length to look for money and throw caution to the wind to display such wealth, given the slightest opportunity.

A pastor was widely criticized some time ago by believers in his city because he decided to celebrate an all-white birthday party for himself in Dubai, spending hundreds of thousands of dollars to organize the party and fly people there. There's nothing wrong with celebrating birthday parties. There's nothing wrong with going to Dubai or any other country. But as ministers of the gospel, and Christians in general, we must be sensitive to the needs of our society. In a society where more than ninety percent of the population live on less than one dollar per day, it would be uncharitable for a minister of Christ to display wealth and opulence of that magnitude.

Now, let's examine some other sources through which the spirit of mammon manifests in the lives of believers and preachers alike.

ACCUMULATING AND LAYING UP EXPENSIVE PETS AND EXOTIC VEHICLES

I've heard of ministers spending millions of dollars to acquire expensive dogs and pets at the expense of suffering members of their churches.

These are expressions of the mammon spirit. Other ministers of the gospel make it a point of duty to include the latest Ferrari in their fleet of cars, just to demonstrate that our God is not a poor God. They pride themselves on the number of powerful and exotic cars they drive. This is terrible and very grievous in the sight of the Lord. We need to do all things with modesty. Of course, there's nothing wrong with driving a good car. But when a Christian minister makes it a point of duty to accumulate expensive cars that aren't needed, or even driven all the time, they are being controlled by the spirit of mammon.

ACCUMULATING AND LAYING UP EXPENSIVE REAL ESTATE

So many Christians and pastors have been accused of wasting church funds on expensive properties. They're not using these properties for any kingdom advancements. They're just accumulating them for personal use and investment purposes.

Now, don't get me wrong. There's nothing wrong with buying houses or investing in real estate. God teaches our hands to make profit. However, it is the manifestation of the spirit of mammon for a Christian or minister of the gospel to have an "accumulating spirit" focused on having the most houses or being named the richest landowner. That is not a kingdom mindset.

When the spirit of mammon is in operation in a person's life, it often expresses itself in subtle ways. Ask anyone doing this and they will be quick to tell you that they're not materialistic. But in their hearts, mammon has taken control of them.

PRIVATE JET SYNDROME

There's nothing wrong with buying, leasing, or renting a private jet. I have never been at the forefront of criticizing those who own one. But not everybody needs one. Not everyone's work requires the use of a private jet. Most people who buy jets haven't worked to a point where their itinerary cannot be supported by the operations of normal airlines.

The cost of purchasing most private jets is in the range of thirty to sixty million dollars, while others are far more. The cost of maintaining the jet is another critical issue that often puts their owners under tremendous pressure. Of course, there are Christian businessmen and women whose businesses are global in nature, and they frequently need to be in different countries for short intervals. Furthermore, buying a personal jet doesn't put these people's finances under strain, and neither will maintaining it affect them in any way. Such people shouldn't be questioned for investing in the purchase of private jets.

There are several Christian ministers whose works have grown to the point where the use of a private jet makes an enormous positive impact on their ability to reach more people for Christ.

A jet is a tool, of course. However, if your decision to buy and own a private jet is born out of a need for additional pleasure, and that pleasure will put pressure on your church members and society at large, you might be opening the door to the spirit of mammon. All over the world, owners of private jets pay billions of dollars yearly to fuel and maintain them. You don't have to own a jet if you actually don't need one. Some can't even sit in business class because they feel like they're above that. If you have the funds, of course you can sit in first class. I'm not being legalistic here, but demonstrating the subtle avenues through which Satan penetrates into the hearts and ministries of God's people.

The spirit of mammon is very subtle, and there is a thin line between what is mammon and what is God. Our focus must always be on the acquisition of resources to extend God's kingdom on earth. We must always see ourselves as channels, not as reservoirs.

Mammon has perils. It ruins ministries and defocuses people from their primary calling. It comes along with the spirit of money worship and idolatry. Many people have lost their vision in life by the influence of mammon.

Here are some of the pitfalls that befall Christians who have been taken over by mammon:

- A high propensity to miss their divine purpose and calling in life.
- A high propensity to worship money.
- A high tendency towards sexual immorality.
- A loss of zeal to pray and study God's word.
- A collapse of the prayer altar at home and in churches.

- A high propensity for pride and arrogance.
- A high propensity to walk perpetually in the flesh.
- Placing unnecessary pressure on family, friends, and church members.
- Breeding an unholy spirit of competition, envy, and jealousy.
- Eroding one's motivation to be kingdom-minded and making the individual money minded.
- Breeding the spirit of corruption in the church and among ministers to the extent that they begin to wine and dine with personalities whom they should actually be influencing to the kingdom of God.
- A high propensity to land a believer or preacher in hell at the end of their life.

Summary of Chapter Ten

1. When the spirit of mammon grips a church or a Christian, the results are terrible. Pastors can go to any length to look for money and throw caution to the wind to display such wealth given the slightest opportunity.
2. In a society where there is a greater proportion of poor people than rich, it would be uncharitable for a minister of Christ to display wealth and opulence.
3. Mammon has perils. It ruins ministries and defocuses people from their primary calling.
4. The spirit of mammon is very subtle, and there is a thin line between what is mammon and what is God. If you're not careful, you can switch from what is God to what is mammon.

CHAPTER ELEVEN

THE MONEY CHANGERS

There is a group of pastors in town these days. They are called "money changers." The first use of this term is found in John 2:14–15. But merely reading this scripture without the operation of the spirit of wisdom and revelation buries the real meaning.

And found in the temple those that sold oxen and sheep and doves, and the changers of money sitting: and when he had made a scourge of small cords, he drove them all out of the temple, and the sheep, and the oxen; and poured out the changers' money, and overthrew the tables. (John 2:14–15)

Our TVs are constantly bombarded with requests for money (or seeds) by pastors across the globe. I have no problem with the act, but with the spirit and motivation behind the requests. Not every request for money on TV is genuinely motivated and inspired by the Spirit of God.

But it's important for us to look inside our churches to find the true meaning of these two words: money changers. Jesus was so angry with these people that He used a whip to chase them out. If Jesus was angry then, He is no less angry today.

Money-changing is an old Jewish act done in the temple at Jerusalem. History tells us that most of the people coming to the temple held the Roman coin, which had a picture of Caesar inscribed on it. Many of them knew this was idolatry and didn't want to give it for their offerings. As such, the act of changing money was very popular. However, Jesus was annoyed—not at the fact that they needed to change their monies to what best suited their giving activities, but that they were doing it in the temple of God.

Many of our temples have been turned into money-changing centres by pastors and ministers. What money-changing means is this: "Give this amount in exchange for this blessing." This has been massively abused. You don't have to give to God for Him to bless you with something. It's faulty theology to teach believers bought with the blood of Jesus that God will always need them to part with money for Him to give them anything. It is wrong and satanic.

Many preachers are guilty of these wrong theologies, and many gullible Christians have failed to confirm the truth behind this act. Of course God can place a condition on people for a specific blessing, but that must be on account of God's instruction. Many preachers now make it to look like God always instructs them to request a special seed from people as a condition for His blessings. Yet many pastors tell their members that God wants a sacrifice from them every Sunday or every week. Many people have been held in bondage by this faulty principle.

I learned my lesson after responding to several calls for giving and nothing came back in return. Watch that language: nothing came back in return. That's what the money-changing spirit breeds among Christians. They become transactionary with God. Instead of walking with God and giving to Him as an act of love, they trade with God. I give you this, you give me that. Of course, I don't regret giving to God, even if He doesn't bless me in return. By sending Jesus to die for me on the cross, He has given me the best gift in life.

In 1 King 17, God asked Elijah to go to the widow of Zarephath. The widow was given a word from the Lord to give her so-called last meal to Elijah and expect a supernatural harvest from God.

And she said, As the Lord thy God liveth, I have not a cake, but an handful of meal in a barrel, and a little oil in a cruse: and, behold, I am gathering two sticks, that I may go in and dress it for me and my son, that we may eat it, and die.

And Elijah said unto her, Fear not; go and do as thou hast said: but make me thereof a little cake first, and bring it unto me, and after make for thee and for thy son. For thus saith the Lord God of Israel, The barrel of meal shall not waste, neither shall the cruse of oil fail, until the day that the Lord sendeth rain upon the earth.
And she went and did according to the saying of Elijah: and she, and he, and her house, did eat many days. (1 Kings 17:12–15)

The problem now is to prove whether or not God is inspiring a particular minister to take special offerings as a condition for a specific blessing. Brother Copeland said emphatically in one of his books that "not every seed must be planted everywhere, and your seed must be sown in the right soil, otherwise, you may get no harvest."[14] He advised that Christians ask God for the place of their harvest prior to giving to any cause. Of course, I'm not suggesting that we shouldn't give regular offerings to our churches, neither am I condemning the act of raising special funds; I am referring to specific cases where a preacher ties your seed to a particular blessing and tells you to do so all the time.

Now, it is very important to draw a line here. An anointed minister of God who carries grace can actually impart blessings on a giver for any need of the giver and God will back it up. The anointing makes the difference. It is possible for a minister of God who carries the anointing of the Holy Spirit to raise offerings and tie them to a specific blessing in the life of the giver and there will be an instant result. I'm careful here not to give an impression that all ministers of God who raise offerings and tie them to specific blessings are false. No, that is not what I'm saying. I am speaking to money-changers. They tie seeds to every need in people's lives. They don't teach grace. They ignore the love of God. They don't raise believers who give to God because they love Him. They raise believers who use their money to sway God to bless them. They are at the extreme end of God's giving principle. These are the people I'm referring to and they are plentiful.

[14] Kenneth Copeland, *Blessed to Be a Blessing* (Fort Worth, TX: Kenneth Copeland Publications, 1997), 48.

Listen, you don't always have to give to God to get your healing. You don't always have to give to God to get a new job. You don't always have to give to God to get a promotion and rise higher in your calling or ministry. The primary thing God needs from you is your heart and obedience to Him all the time. However, God can place a demand on your finances for a specific project at hand. Once you obey God and release that seed, you can never miss the reward.

I have experienced this in my own life and ministry. While I was living in South Africa for a particular period, I was practically living from hand to mouth. I was jobless and had no one to help me. I was then inspired by God to sow the last cash on me and a set of cufflinks to the church. In less than three months, my life was transformed. I got a scholarship to study an MBA program in a leading UK institution. Everything turned around.

I began to depend on instruction for other needs I had, and failed woefully. I applied for a visa to another country and sowed a seed towards it. I used the seed principle indiscriminately, not knowing that I was already shifting into the realm of money-changing. I sowed a special seed yet was denied the visa.

A lot of people have complained to me about the activities of some pastors on TBN and Daystar. Some of them have been taken over completely by this money-changing spirit, and they don't know it. Some ask people for money in exchange for a cloth and an anointed paper. Money is being traded for power.

Jesus told the apostles,

Heal the sick, cleanse the lepers, raise the dead, cast out devils: freely ye have received, freely give. (Matthew 10:8)

What part of the above scripture is difficult to understand? Anyone who asks you to send money in exchange for healing cloth is certainly not sent by Jesus. You must not respond to such a request. Let me tell you something: it is possible for you to send money to a pastor in exchange for power and you will still receive healing. Never test the authenticity of a minister of God by proofs, but rather by fruits.

Fruits don't deceive for a long time; proofs can be faked. Satan can manipulate proofs. The Bible says, *"Wherefore by their fruits ye shall know them"* (Matthew 7:20). Not by their proofs! I am referring to the fruits of the spirit, such as love, joy, and peace as spelled out in Galatians 5.

It is possible for a man to be inspired by God to sow a seed into a ministry for a desired harvest and God will grant the request. Faith is so powerful that it's actually possible to drag anything out of the hand of God by faith. There are no rules involved in this matter. What we should be primary concerned with is doing things out of love all the time. We must develop into disciples and not remain ordinary churchgoers. Disciples are so loyal to their masters that whether the master helps them or not, they are forever sold out to him. Secondly, we must test every spirit and recognize that unless we can accurately decipher the voice of the Holy Spirit, no one must force us to give in exchange for any blessing. Lastly, we must also respond to personal promptings of faith.

You can be told by God to sow into a ministry or project for a miracle, and if you obey those promptings God can bless you tremendously. I have experienced this on several occasions. Some years back, a pastor came to Canada and asked unmarried women to sow a special seed towards getting husbands in seven days. They did, but none of them got husbands—and the preacher ran away with their money.

There are so many cases of believers who were robbed of their houses, cars, and other valuables by pastors who told them to sow seeds for desired harvests. We must test every spirit. The money-changing spirit is from Satan, and that spirit's twin brother is mammon. It is different from the prompting of the spirit to give for a desired harvest. It is also different from our regular commitment to our local churches in tithes and offerings and other special donations.

The following chart shows the differences between the money-changing spirit and the Holy Spirit's promptings for giving.

The Money-Changing Spirit	The Holy Spirit
You can never prosper if you don't give material things to God.	You don't have to give God material things to prosper.
If you don't give your way to the top, you can't get to the top.	You can get to the top without giving. Giving is not the only principle of success.
You must always tie your seed to your harvest, otherwise you can't harvest anything from God.	You don't always have to tie seeds to desired harvests. God can still bless His children without them sowing seeds for such blessings.
If you need God's anointing, you must sow material things into the anointing.	You don't have to sow any material seed to be anointed by God.
If you don't tithe, life will be tight for you.	You should tithe to God. But even if by mistake you have failed to tithe, God can still bless you because He loves you.

PERILS OF THE MONEY-CHANGING SPIRIT

- It doesn't raise disciples out of Christians. It raises Christians who don't love God because of who He is, but because of what He gives.
- It repositions the priority of believers on money as the only means for pleasing God.
- It can impoverish people.
- It can build a spirit of competition, bitterness, envy, and jealousy among believers.
- It engenders a transactionary relationship between believers and God.
- It undermines and diminishes the influence of Christ's works of grace and makes believers rely on the works of their hands as conditions to get God to bless them.

God is calling out His people to arise from their slumber and become true disciples who truly love Him and are motivated by this love in their relationship with Him all the time.

Money-changing in our churches is offensive to God, and very sinful as well. If Jesus used a whip, He won't use anything lesser at this critical hour in the history of the church.

Money is not the most powerful weapon. Love is the most potent force. Let His love, which has been shed abroad in our hearts by the Holy Ghost, reposition us into our true positions in Christ.

BUYERS AND SELLERS

Jesus wasn't only upset with the money-changers, but also with buyers and sellers. Some pastors don't actually ask people to sow a seed for a desired harvest. What they do is to milk their church members by openly selling the power of God to them in the form of anointed handkerchiefs and oils. If these materials were sold to people in ordinary shops without a so-called anointing, this wouldn't be an issue. But these materials aren't just the object of sales. It's the power that they carry, and that is where the problem is.

You cannot sell the power of God in any form. Buying and selling can be subtle in appearance. Truly, there is nothing sinful in a church having bookshops or retail outlets for the sale of books and other materials that can help a believer to grow. The problem arises from declaring certain materials as anointed and asking people to deliberately pay for them so the power on them can be transferred to them. It is occultic and satanic. These practices are common with witch doctors in many parts of Africa, and it is unfortunate that many Christians have unconsciously been deceived by their pastors to patronize these terrible practices.

Incredible acts? I assure you, these are common occurrences in many churches in Africa.

SUMMARY OF CHAPTER ELEVEN

1. You don't have to give money to God all the time for Him to bless you.
2. It is a faulty theology to teach believers who were bought with the blood of Jesus that God needs them to part with money for Him to give them anything.

3. The primary thing God needs from you is your heart and obedience. However, God can place a demand on your finances for a specific project at hand. Once you obey God and release that seed, you can never miss the reward.

4. Never test the authenticity of a minister of God by proofs, but by fruits. Fruits (the ones listed in Galatians 5) don't deceive for a long time. Proofs can be faked. Satan can manipulate proofs.

5. The money-changing spirit is from Satan, and the spirit's twin brother is mammon. It is different from the prompting of the spirit to give for a desired harvest.

CHAPTER TWELVE

MINISTRY SUCCESS AND WEALTH
ACCUMULATION

I became a Christian in the early 80s, a period when most pastors and those called into the fivefold ministry didn't measure their success by worldly acquisitions. I give thanks to God that I knew Christ at this period. If I had been born again in this present decade, I would have been swept by the current wind of materialism. We now live in a generation where preachers measure their success by many mundane things.

Given my more than thirty years of relationship with God, and many preachers, I have come to identify the following measures of ministry success.

- The number of members in your church.
- The financial strength of your church.
- The number of famous people associated with the church.
- The presence of the church on radio, TV, or other mass or social media.
- The number and type of construction and real estate projects of the church.
- The type of cars driven by pastors and members of the church.
- The ownership of private jets, universities, and other capital assets.

The list is endless. Of course, some of the items listed above are measures of progress. I don't mean to categorize these items as sinful. In fact, none of them are sinful. They are all laudable achievements if one's ultimate motive is to expand the kingdom of God. However, this is not so with every church. Many pastors who crave these things have no iota of motive for expanding the kingdom of God. This has opened the door for Satan to hijack the vision of many preachers to the extent that unholy competitions for things are the order of the day.

WHAT IS THE MEANING OF SUCCESS IN LIFE AND MINISTRY?

But what does it mean to be a successful minister? Ministry doesn't only refer to the preaching of the gospel; it covers every ministry office God has called us into, be it academics, business, education, sports, or arts and entertainment. What does success mean to us? Not understanding what true success means, and what it is to God, might be the main reason for the abuse of wealth and material prosperity in the church and among Christians.

Success in any endeavour stems from the following;
• Identifying a goal or target.
• Understanding the goal or target in terms of minimum expectations.
• Meeting those minimum expectations to the best of your ability.

In other words, I cannot just score any mark in an examination and claim to have passed the paper. In the world of academics, the department regulating the exam sets the minimum passing grade against which the performance of all students will be judged. Thus, if fifty percent is set up as the minimum passing grade, everyone who scores forty-nine percent and below has not passed.

Isn't that simple analogy instructive? What should be my primary focus in the fulfillment of my goals and objectives?
• To identify the content of my assignment.
• To identify the passing grades for my assignment.
• To work towards meeting those grades as well as I can.

Unfortunately, many people don't understand this simple concept. They're pursuing ministry success using their own standards. They forget that *"every one of us shall give account of himself to God"* (Romans 14:12).

For we must all appear before the judgment seat of Christ; that every one may receive the things done in his body, according to that he hath done, whether it be good or bad. (2 Corinthians 5:10)

God is the final tutor who will mark my examination sheet, and by every means possible I must write the examination of destiny by His grading standard. In other words, success in life or ministry entails identifying your life assignment, identifying the terms of the assignment, identifying the passing grade, and committing yourself to finishing the assignment in line with those standards. Simply put, success in life or ministry can be summed up in one sentence: you must be obedient to the giver of the assignment.

WHAT IS THE BIBLICAL DESCRIPTION OF SUCCESS?

His lord said unto him, Well done, thou good and faithful servant: thou hast been faithful over a few things, I will make thee ruler over many things: enter thou into the joy of thy lord. (Matthew 25:21)

This story is dead on target. Two phrases are particularly striking: "well done" and faithful servant." The Message bible makes it easier to understand.

The one given five thousand dollars showed him how he had doubled his investment. His master commended him: "Good work! You did your job well. From now on be my partner." (Matthew 25:21, The Message, emphasis added)

You did your job well. That is success per excellence. Notice that the servant didn't assess his own work. It is possible for a man to think he is successful while he continues wasting time on vanities. However, if a man understands the terms of his assignment well, it is still possible to know whether he is doing the right thing. This all depends on the strength of the relationship between him and God.

Secondly, the master identifies a person's faithfulness. Derek Prince, in one of his sermons, drew my attention to this verse. In the story, the master is concerned about both success and faithfulness. In other words, it's possible to be successful and not faithful. However, you can't be faithful to God and not be successful. We should therefore pursue faithfulness first; success will come naturally.

From the scriptures we've just examined, we can see that God's standard for assessing any ministry stems from the following;

- You must have a relationship with God. You cannot be unsaved and claim to have succeeded in life. Regardless of how committed you are to your life's vision and assignment, if you are not saved, you will be lost forever in hell.
- You must identify that you are a servant and God is the master. This implies that you must never think higher of yourself than you should. You must know that you are not in charge. Someone is waiting to assess your work when you die. In other words, you must live a life of accountability at all times.
- You must identify your life's purpose and assignment without any iota of doubt.
- You must identify and understand the terms of your assignment. This includes the place of your assignment, the scope of your assignment, the specific outcomes of your assignment (in terms of time, quantity, and quality), and the final grade of your assignment.

Did you see any mention of the size of car you drive or the kind of house you live in? If you're measuring your success based on those elements, you are in grave danger! Regrettably, a lot of Christians are busy with the wrong assignments—and they will be scored a zero on the last day. Do you want to labour on earth and get to heaven to be given a zero score? What a terrible day it will be for many preachers and Christians who have spent their whole lives doing things they were not sent to the world to do.

Dr. Myles Munroe once said that the biggest disaster we can face in life isn't actually death, but living without purpose.[15]

---

[15] Dr. Myles Monroe, *In Pursuit of Purpose* (Shippensburg, PA: Destiny Image, 1992).

Perhaps the materialism in the lives of many preachers is related to their lack of direction. They don't know their exact purpose in ministry and are thus living a confused life.

Every character in the Bible who succeeded by God's standard had one thing in common: obedience. I don't know of any biblical character who was pronounced successful by God outside of their implicit obedience to God. David, Abraham, Daniel, Paul, Jacob, Isaac, Isaiah, and of course the Lord Jesus... they all identified their assignment and purpose in God and obeyed it to the fullest. Conversely, those who failed did not obey God. Some, like Saul, actually knew their assignments but did not obey. But whether or not you know your assignment, you will still suffer the consequences of not obeying God. In a court of law, ignorance of the law is not an excuse for breaking the law.

One of the most fearful scriptures to me clearly explains what I mean:

And that servant, which knew his lord's will, and prepared not himself, neither did according to his will, shall be beaten with many stripes. But he that knew not, and did commit things worthy of stripes, shall be beaten with few stripes. For unto whomsoever much is given, of him shall be much required: and to whom men have committed much, of him they will ask the more. (Luke 12:47–48)

This is the most fearful scriptures in the New Testament. Whether or not you know God's purpose for your life, you are not excused from the consequences of not obeying God. Simply put, complete obedience to God is the number one hallmark of success in life and ministry.

> ...COMPLETE OBEDIENCE TO GOD IS THE NUMBER ONE HALLMARK OF SUCCESS IN LIFE AND MINISTRY.

I therefore submit to all reading this book that every act of disobedience to the terms of your calling and ministry reduces the success of your life and ministry. It is therefore regrettable to see how many people, including pastors, crave after the wrong things. I wonder how buying houses all around the world, accumulating a fleet of expensive cars, flying from nation to nation, and fraternizing with political leaders can equal success.

In the fulfillment of your life's mission, material things including money, relationships, and resources will be needed. If you are faithful and serious with your purpose, those things will be naturally attracted to you.

As I mentioned earlier, your primary focus should be directed towards becoming an expert at your assignment. Focusing on accumulating wealth is a strategy of the devil to derail you from your purpose. You cannot be running after money and fulfilling your purpose at the same time. If care is not taken, the spirit of mammon will enter you and you will lose focus on your main mission on earth and waste your life on the acquisition of that which will not be rewarded. God doesn't reward the accumulation of wealth; He only rewards the fulfillment of a person's assignment.

It is, however, possible for the fulfillment of an assignment to open the door to wealth. Your heart must be driven towards your assignment and not towards wealth. I strongly admonish all those reading this book to reorganize their focus. Stop wasting your time on things for which you will not be rewarded. Jesus makes it clear:

And he said unto them, Take heed, and beware of covetousness: for a man's life consisteth not in the abundance of the things which he possesseth. (Luke 12:15)

Then Jesus said to them, "Watch out! Guard yourself against all kinds of greed. After all, one's life isn't determined by one's possessions, even when someone is very wealthy." (Luke 12:15, CEB)

Speaking to the people, he went on, "Take care! Protect yourself against the least bit of greed. Life is not defined by what you have, even when you have a lot." (Luke 12:15, The Message)

Your material possessions don't move God an inch.

In conclusion, the only requirement for success in life or ministry is complete obedience to God. You must identify God's assignment and the full details of the assignment and work faithfully to fulfill those details as much as you are empowered by God to do so.

SUMMARY OF CHAPTER TWELVE

1. Complete obedience to God is the number one hallmark of success in life and ministry.
2. Success in any endeavour stems from the following: identifying a goal or target, understanding the goal or target in terms of minimum expectations, and meeting those minimum expectations to the best of your ability.
3. It is possible for a man to think he is successful while wasting time on vanities. However, if a man understands the terms of his assignment well, it is still possible to know whether or not he is doing the right thing.
4. It is possible to be successful and not faithful. However, you can't be faithful to God and not be successful.
5. Ignorance of your purpose doesn't excuse you from the consequences of not fulfilling your purpose.
6. Every character in the Bible who succeeded by God's standard had one thing in common: obedience.
7. Focusing on accumulating wealth is a strategy of the devil to derail you from your life's purpose. The two don't work together. You cannot be running after money and fulfilling your purpose at the same time.

CONCLUSION

Let us hear the conclusion of the whole matter: Fear God, and keep his commandments: for this is the whole duty of man. (Ecclesiastes 12:13)

I love the above scripture with my whole heart. Even Solomon, in his unregenerated state, was permitted by God to understand what is the nucleus of the whole existence of mankind. What Solomon says here is simple: everything revolves round obedience. Just identify your life's assignment and commit yourself to obeying God to the fullest in that area and you will win the heart of God.

Silver and gold belong to our God. What would you as a parent not do to bless and help your son who constantly does what you want him to do? Every man is made by his obedience or wrecked by his disobedience. Regardless of your position in society, God's number one criterion is obedience. Whether you're a preacher or just a good Christian, you must seek to always understand God's standard and instructions as they relate to your life, and you must commit yourself to obeying them.

I always cry to the Holy Spirit to help me in the pursuit of my calling. I pray a very fearful prayer. I ask God to close any door if it will take me away from my assignment. We are sometimes influenced by our environment and relationships to the extent that we tend to be distracted. Since I'm a man and am prone to mistakes, I engage the Holy Spirit to guide and direct my affairs to the centre of God's will at all times.

The assistant to Kenneth Hagin was once asked in a TVV interview why he refused to start his own ministry in spite of his level of wisdom and anointing. His answer still baffles me: "It is better to be number two in the plan of God than to be number one in your own plan." He simply meant that, based on his assignment and life's instructions from God, he was supposed to be Hagin's assistant.

Personally, I have asked God why He allowed and directed me to serve in different ministries around the world, while He has anointed me so powerfully to teach and preach His words. Between 1984 and 2005, I served with three different ministries in Nigeria. Between 2005 and 2006, I served with another ministry in South Africa. Between 2006 and 2010, I served with a ministry in Scotland. Between 2010 and 2011, I served with a ministry in Cambridge. Between 2011 and 2014, I served with a ministry in Ontario, Canada, and between 2014 and 2016, I served with another ministry in Canada. During these periods, we started our own ministry on a part-time basis, but with no instruction to detach from these other ministries. We published books, hosted conferences, and trained people—all with no church presence.

More than thirty-two years of service have now passed. God then came to me to launch a new church. For many years, I asked God why He kept pushing me around. I now understand better. My reward in heaven is based on my work of the last thirty-two years, plus my work in the next fifty years if Jesus tarries. My life is like an examination with two sections. Have you written such exams before? Had I not completed Section A, I would never have been asked to begin Section B.

Many of us are busy doing things that will be consumed by fire. The fire of God will test our work at the end of the day.

Every man's work shall be made manifest: for the day shall declare it, because it shall be revealed by fire; and the fire shall try every man's work of what sort it is. If any man's work abide which he hath built thereupon, he shall receive a reward. If any man's work shall be burned, he shall suffer loss: but he himself shall be saved; yet so as by fire. (1 Corinthians 3:13–15)

If you have been taken over by the spirit of mammon, it will be a sad outcome. You must turn around and run back to God. If you don't know any other thing but material and financial accomplishments, you still have time. Turn to God in repentance. Develop a kingdom mindset. Look for opportunities to make an impact on the poor and less privileged in your sphere of influence. Take your trust away from money and material possessions. Live a kingdom-minded life. If you are a pastor and have derailed, run back to God. If you are pursuing bread and fish, change your focus and start running after fire. Become fired up in your life's purpose and watch how the fish and bread run after you.

God and mammon are two opposite entities. You can't be possessed by the spirit of God and at the same time be possessed by the spirit of mammon. You cannot serve God and mammon. That is the very heart of this book, and I hope that you have been tremendously blessed by it.

If you are not yet saved, you must take a strong and quick step to become God's own dear son. Kindly repeat these words:

Lord Jesus, I believe You are the son of God. I believe You came into the world to die for my sins. I believe You died, rose again on the third day, and are coming back again. Come and forgive me all my sins and live in my heart. I accept You into my life as my personal Lord and Saviour. From today, I am born again.

Next, you should seek a Bible-believing church and start fellowshiping with the people of God. You should also get a Bible with the Old and New Testaments and begin to read from John 1.

For further counsel, do not hesitate to contact us:

Pastor Ayo Akerele
Voice of the Watchmen Ministries (Rhema For Living Assembly)
7198 Frontier Ridge
Mississauga, ON, L5N 7R2

Website: www.rhemaforliving.org
Email: ayoakerele@hotmail.com or info@vowministries.org or
rhemaforliving2016@gmail.com
Telephone: (647) 477-9472 or (647) 704-7453

Ayo Akerele is also the senior pastor of Rhema For Living Assembly in Toronto, a fast growing congregation of firebrand believers.
rhemaforliving2016@gmail.com

Coming Soon
The Hunters and the Flock Keeper
Not For Price Not For Reward
Finding and Fulfilling God's Plan for Your Life

PUBLICATIONS

In the last two years, VOW Ministries (Rhema For Living Assembly) has published four books that have reached Africa, Europe, Asia, Australia and New Zealand, and North America. Some of the current titles in print include:

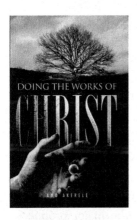

DOING THE WORKS OF CHRIST

Many who claim to be Christians are not Christians. Most did not die to self at the new birth, but merely fainted. This book teaches us that to do the works of Christ, we need faith. Faith on the other hand is provoked by revelation, while revelation is the product of deep fellowship and intimacy with God in His word and in prayer. Since everything produces after its kind, the child of God must of necessity live like God, influencing lives and performing signs and wonders by default.

REDISCOVERING THE POWER OF SPIRITUALFRUITFULNESS

This book uncovers the practical meaning of fruits, seeds and leaves as they relate to Christian lives. It basically emphasizes that in no other generation is the need for Christians to bear fruits in the Spirit as critical like our present generation. The value of this book is hinged to the fact that our impact as Christians in this dark world remains a mirage without a conscious effort to be spiritually fruitful.

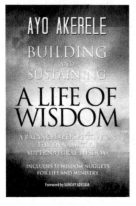

BUILDING AND SUSTAINING A LIFE OF WISDOM

This book uncovers the mystery in the wisdom of God. According to the book, nothing beautifies destiny like the wisdom of God. It is a winner in any contest of life. There is no issue of life that has the capacity to resist the impact of the wisdom of God. Men and women who have made significant positive and sustainable impacts in our world are noted for unusual demonstration of supernatural wisdom. Whether it is in ministry or in the secular world, nothing significant can be achieved without the wisdom of God. Regardless of colour, race and background, God's wisdom makes stars out of anybody. The book summarises that the impact of the church of Christ in this end time is at the mercy of the Spirit of Wisdom.

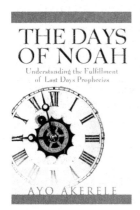

THE DAYS OF NOAH

This book has a prophetic voice. It emphasises that at no other time in history has humanity moved closer to eternity. Throughout the pages of this book, all the major prophecies of the last 4000 years that have been fulfilled in our contemporary world were uncovered and referenced. The captivating nature of the book dwells on the detailed description of the agenda of Satan in this end time as revealed in contemporary events of our world and secondly on the detailed description of the agenda and move of God in this end time. This book clearly presents the major attributes of men and women of the days of Noah and how their lifestyle is playing out in a 21st century world. It concludes that "we are now living in the 21st century days of Noah".

CPSIA information can be obtained
at www.ICGtesting.com
Printed in the USA
LVOW01s0403161216
517507LV00004BA/6/P